BURNLEY COTTON MILLS

BURNLEY COTTON MILLS

BY JACK NADIN

Frontispiece: The upper image shows the cotton mill chimneys in Burnley (courtesy of the Briercliffe Society). The lower shows Albion Mill of Exmouth Street, Burnley.

First published in 2008

Reprinted in 2012

The History Press
The Mill, Brimscombe Port,
Stroud, Gloucestershire, GL5 2QG
www.thehistorypress.co.uk

British Library Cataloguing in Publication Data.
A catalogue record for this book is available from the British Library.

ISBN 978 0 7524 4659 2

Typesetting and origination by The History Press Ltd
Printed and bound in Great Britain

CONTENTS

INTRODUCTION

Take a close look around Burnley today, and you will be able to see just how many old mills remain. Many of course have been put to different use, and many more still have gone forever. But there is no mistaking the fact that Burnley was, and still is in many ways, a mill town. There is no way of telling now just what Burnley would have become had it not been for cotton weaving and cotton spinning; it was the town's 'staple industry' for almost 200 years. Without cotton, in all probability, Burnley as we know it would never have existed: without its intervention, it would probably have remained an agricultural village. Instead, Burnley progressed forward and became the cotton weaving capital of the world. 'We wove for home use before breakfast and for the rest of the world afterwards', it was said: 63 per cent of the working population of Burnley were working in connection with cotton weaving or cotton spinning, in 1929, the heyday of town's cotton industry.

Following this, there was a steady decline in the industry, mainly brought about by cheap foreign imports. In 1938, there were 43 per cent of the working population in the cotton industry. By 1950, it was down to just 29 per cent, and this was despite an attempt to increase home productivity following the Second World War; 'Britain's bread hung by Lancashire's thread' was the phrase coined the Minister of Labour, Mr George Isaac's, at a visit to the Burnley's Mechanic's Institute on 21 February 1947. This still showed the importance of the cotton industry and its contribution to national wealth.

In retrospect we might have contributed to our own downfall, for Burnley was also a large producer of looms. These were exported to other countries, which in turn began to turn out cotton and cotton goods at a rate much cheaper than we could produce it. But, having said that, if we hadn't produced the looms, then someone else would have! Following the 1950s, there was an even sharper decline in the cotton and associated industries, as newer industries, particularly engineering, emerged in the town.

Many mills, however, remain today, as the testimony to 'King Cotton'; and are now part of our industrial heritage. I have also tried to include many of the mills and factories now long gone: they were still part of our proud and rich industrial past. This is not meant to be a comprehensive or detailed study of the history of Burnley's mills – space doesn't allow that – but more to relate what remains, if anything, today as industrial archaeology in the town, with a brief history where applicable. This publication only covers the cotton mills, weaving and spinning, and those connected with textiles and worsted mills. Modern mills and factories have not been included, for they lack both history and architectural 'beauty' of the older, dare I say, 'dark satanic mills'. There is often confusion when researching old mills: most are officially named, but often show up in other references named after the owner at that particular time. Mills of course change owners, and what might be named after one owner, might again be named something completely different a few decades later.

Mills and factories in Burnley first began to make an appearance from around the late 1730s. The town wasn't chosen at random; a major factor was the damp climate: winds and rains sweeping in from the west quickly condensed on the approach to the Pennine hills and Old Pendle itself. Another major factor was the Leeds and Liverpool Canal, besides which many of the mills were situated, for obvious transport reasons.

In the early days, work at the mills and factories was far from ideal. The crude machines were crowded together, there were few precautions against fire, the only light was a flickering candle or at best gas light. The hours were long, often twelve or eighteen hours a day. Some mill owners allowed an hour for dinner, but mostly it was work and eat while you stood by your loom or spindles. Child labour was common, even in the best-kept mills and factories. One Burnley lad in the Salford district of town regularly worked an eighteen-hour day in 1820. Even the very young, the infants, are reported to have been carried to the mills on their fathers' backs, still half asleep, to supplement the family income, and kept working by the strap of the overlooker. Father, wife, sons and daughter often worked together at the looms, a tradition that remained for many years. Children under the age of nine years were forbidden to work under an Act of 1833, but it was not uncommon to hide the underaged in sacks and bales should word get around that an inspector was 'on tour' in the district. Even in the year 1867, it was remarked that a large number of pauper children were often brought into Burnley from other towns to provide cheap labour for the factories. One Burnley master even boasted that the beds of his 'apprentices' were never cold: as one batch moved out to go to the mill, another came from the mill to take his place in the bed.

It wasn't uncommon either for the master to be at the mill before the worker, and anyone late was sent home without pay, and perhaps even fined. Accommodation was as wretched as the workers themselves. A dozen or more women and children, as well as adult males, might occupy a single cottage-type dwelling, with no running water, no sanitary arrangements and no through ventilation. Drunkenness and violence was common, even excepted. Conditions did improve, albeit slowly, but for many years the hours were long and conditions by today's standards would be totally unacceptable. In 1875 the hours of work for the mill and factory workers were reduced to fifty-six and a half hours per week, and by the turn of the nineteenth century, the mill engine was stopped at 11.30 a.m. on Saturdays. Not until 1947 was the forty-five-hour week introduced, but part-timers at the mills are still within living memory; a system finally abolished in 1920. This is the darker side of Burnley's industrial past – happily, times have changed. All that remains of those dark days are the great mills and factories, built from the sweat and labour of Burnley men and womenfolk now long gone. It might be true that a number of manufacturers left behind something for the Burnley folk to enjoy, notably the Thompson, and Thornber families, but most took their wealth with them. The great memorials and monuments at the bottom end of the Municipal Cemetery might testify to their wealth, but death, as always had the monopoly – 'there are no pockets in shrouds', as the old Lancashire saying goes. Their legacy remains with us today as the industrial heritage in the town, just another part, but a very important part of Burnley's history.

I am grateful for the advice and help from a number of sources, in particular local historians James Howell and Ken Spencer, who placed me back on the right track a number of times. The staff at Burnley Reference Library, and Susan Hartley and Janice Bell for their help. Thanks to Roger Frost and the Briercliffe Society for the use of a number of photographs, all of which add to the interest of the book. Mike Townsend at Towneley Hall. Special thanks go to my partner in life, my wife, Rita, for all her patience – despite her illness – while researching this project.

BURNLEY MILLS

ALBERT MILL, CANNING STREET, BURNLEY

The Albert Mill was on Canning Street, going towards the Stoneyholme area, and was being worked in 1879 by Richard Hardman, cotton manufacturer. Richard Hardman was born at Spotland, near Rochdale, around 1829, and at that time he was running the Albert Mill he lived at No. 62 Albion Street. Albert Mill was also worked by Lancaster's in the 1920s, but was owned by George Keighley, (of the huge Bankhouse Ironworks). The mill was a weaving mill, consisting of three sheds, warehouses and stores. Shed No.1 was the largest covering 2,000 yards of floor space. The No. 2 Shed had 900 yards of floor space, and No. 3 had 800. The warehouses and store had a floor space of 970 yards, and all the floors had an average height of 12ft. All the buildings had flagstone flooring, and were stone built, and the site contained a private reservoir at its northern end. The mill was powered in the mid-1930s by two Lancashire boilers, which provided the steam for a 300hp compound steam engine. The Thornhill Manufacturing Co. in 1934 was working Albert Shed; however, all its 800 looms were stopped. The site of Albert Mill Canning Street has been taken over by modern development, including in part the Asda car park. It appears that the Co-op garage used part of the sheds on Canning Street at some later date. I seem to remember the Co-op vans using the garages here in the early 1960s.

ALBERT MILL, TRAFALGAR STREET, BURNLEY

Named after Queen Victoria's husband (one of a number locally), this mill was built around 1870, for Thomas Pomfret, as a cotton-spinning mill, according to a number of sources. However, Bennett, in his *History of Burnley* Vol. III, page 182 says, 'Varley and Pomfret's Mill near Varley Street (Which was off Trafalgar Street) was built about 1830'. Thomas Pomfret lived at Olive Mount with his wife Susanne and son John Varley Pomfret; Thomas Pomfret died in 1897. The Albert mill was offered for sale by auction on Wednesday 2 October 1929, at the Bull Hotel on Manchester Road, along with the Trafalgar Shed close by. Dexter's Paints Ltd now use part of the mill premises today. The buildings at Albert Mill had a total floor space of over 3,600 square yards. It comprised of two four-storey mills, each measuring 90ft by 50ft, with engine house, boiler houses and other outbuildings. Much of the former cotton mill survives to this day.

ALBION MILL, (ALSO KNOWN AS HARGEAVES), EXMOUTH STREET, BURNLEY

Exmouth Street is the street almost under the Centenary Way flyover on Finsleygate. This is a typical cotton-spinning mill of several floors. Spinning mills in general differed from weaving mills in the number of floors, the latter using heavier machinery, limiting it to just one, or maybe two floors. Spinning mills however, used lighter machines and could be worked on a number of floors. In recent years, various car repair firms and garages used the former Albion Mill on the Finsley Gate side, but now it is more or less derelict. The Albion Mill was also known as 'Hargreaves', which was a cotton mill in 1851 and included those buildings around the corner on what is today Cooper Street, but formerly known as Barrack Street, from the time there used to be a barracks around here. The mills on this side, Cooper Street side, are the oldest – dating from the mid-1820s – and may have taken their name from Henry Hargreaves, who was listed as a cotton manufacturer and spinner at Lane Bridge, the old name for this area of town. The Albion Mill was working on Barracks Street in 1868, by Charles Leopold Schwabe, 'Cotton spinner and manufacturer'. At some time the Albion Mill had two beam engines, each of 50hp. Many years later, in 1944, the mill was taken over by a firm of sack and bag makers, known as J.E. Simpson and Sons. A serious fire there in October 1986 caused damage to the value of £25,000; fortunately the machines were on the other side of the mill and they were able to carry on as normal. Today the mill presents a sorry sight in its derelict state and its future looks uncertain: indeed in 2005 an application was received to demolish the buildings in Cooper Street for housing, but this was refused.

ALBION MILL, COTTON STREET, WHITTLEFIELD, BURNLEY

The Albion Mill was sandwiched between the Cairo Mill and Pendle View Shed, on Cotton Street, and has now been demolished. Nothing remains of Albion Mill at the time of writing; modern housing has now taken its place. The mill dated from around 1861. In 1879, Albion Mill was being worked by Thomas Henry Lomas, and Edward Lord, probably on the 'room and power' basis. The earliest mention of room and power is in a Burnley mill in the year 1855. Robert Pickles, and George Pomfret were also here in 1879. By 1887 the firm of Bullock and Trelfall were working at the Albion Mill with 392 looms, and were making among other things umbrella cloth. There was a serious incident just before Christmas 1884 when there was a fracture of the flywheel at the mill which threw over 400 workers out of work. The cotton weavers must have really struggled that year for presents for the children and to survive a terrible winter. In later years the mill was worked by Simpson and Baldwin in 1923 and 1945. This firm also operated the Tunnel Street Mill, and both mills worked 1,688 looms. Connected with this firm were William Baldwin, John Starkie Baldwin, Frank Simpson and J.E. Myers. There was a terrible fire at the Albion Mill in January 1897; two weavers were killed in the conflagration.

ASHFIELD SHED, CALDERVALE ROAD, BURNLEY

Although some distance from Ashfield, this shed survives today, worked as John Spencer's, (Textiles) Ltd on the little bit of Caldervale Road that is still left. It was in 1871 that John Spencer started in business along with his son John, and John's brother, at the Waterloo shed on Trafalgar Street, with just 110 looms. The business grew substantially however over the years, and at one stage had over 2,000 looms, but along with the rest of the textile industry in the county, it ran in to hard times – the days of 'King Cotton' were coming to an end. The firm was eventually wound up in 1971, but a family interest was maintained by the name of the new company John Spencer (Textiles) Ltd. The Ashfield Mill was being worked by William Dugdale in the late 1870s, but actually dates from around 1861. The mill, however, was largely rebuilt following a disastrous fire in 1991 and worked by F. Parkinson and Co. in 1923, who also operated the Caldervale Mills next door.

The Ashfield Mill Co. Ltd owned the mill in the mid-1930s, and it was built as a weaving shed, with a floor space, including warehousing, of 5,090 yards. One Lancashire boiler with a local Proctor's automatic stoker, and a Green's economiser provided the steam for a horizontal steam engine installed in 1914. The engine was fitted with a rope flywheel drive. A date stone can be seen fitted, or rather re-fitted, above the main doorway to the mill offices, and bears the date 1861. Ashfield Shed had at one time 43,000 spindles (throstle and mule) and 700 looms. The erection of the Ashfield Shed was untimely, being built just before the American Civil War, and the Cotton Famine that followed. It was soon declared bankrupt due to £5,000 of debt. The 'Calder Vale Self-Help Co.' which was formed in April 1888 took over the 1,000 looms at the Ashfield Shed from J. H. Whitaker. The manager was James Whitaker, the son of the late owner. It too went bankrupt in 1889, to the great disappointment of workers watching these interesting experiments in co-operative ownership and management. The main reason for the failure was the depression in trade and the resulting low prices. The present building is the one rebuilt after the fire, and the office section is constructed as the original in dressed stone, while the rear of the building is of more modern sheet steel and girder-work. The mill was offered for sale on Wednesday 17 June 1891 at the Bull Hotel, Manchester Road, Burnley, and described as follows:

All that modern weaving shed called 'Ashfield Mill' Burnley holding 896 patent power looms. The buildings are of stone. The motive power consists of one three flued steam boiler by Layfield, 1886 fitted with proctor's Patent Stokers. Pair of beam engines by Woods and McNaughted. Horizontal steam engine 5 inch cylinder, 10 inch stroke, Green Economiser. Mill gearing, shafting, steam, gas and water pipes. A good supply of water for driving purposes from a goit on the River Calder, charge for which is included in the rent. The land forming the site contains 4,571 yards and is subject to a yearly ground rent of £55 6s…

BANK HALL MILL, DANESHOUSE ROAD, BURNLEY

The Bank Hall Mill, or Bank Hall Shed, is unusual for a Burnley mill; a red-brick weaving shed, with northern light roof. The mill still survives and can be seen from the Canal Bridge on Daneshouse Road on the right-hand side (Colne Road side) of the bridge. Today George Cormack (Waterbarn) Ltd works the mill, a firm of felt manufacturers. It's not known exactly when the mill was erected – it's not shown on a map of 1910, or 1912, but is shown on a map of 1931. It must therefore have been erected between these two dates.

BANKFIELD MILL, CURZON STREET/BANKHOUSE STREET, BURNLEY

A mill established as a small cotton factory in 1820 by William Hopwood and William Pollard. John Barnes and Son is listed working the Bankfield mill in 1848, and in 1868, and interestingly at the latter date the address is Parsonage Street, the old name for this part of Curzon Street. Bennett, in his *History of Burnley,* related that, 'The stench near Bankfield Mill, where a dam had been constructed, made it impossible to cross Curzon Street Bridge and rendered life unbearable in houses near the present Market Square'. The John Barnes,

Bank Hall Mill.

mentioned above, was born near Haslingden on 2 June 1808. The family moved to Burnley around 1827 and began in business in a cotton factory at Pendle Bottom. John and his brother George moved to the Bankfield Mill in 1842. John Barnes was mayor of the town in 1862-63, 1869-70 and in 1870-71, and lived at Reedley Hall, known locally as 'Barnes Manor' or 'Barnes Hall'. He died in June 1878. Sixty-one-year-old Geoffrey Hoyle, who had worked at Bankfield Mill for over seventeen years, was sadly killed in a hoist accident there in January 1919. By the mid-1920s the mill was occupied by a number of firms, including Smith's tobacco works, King's boot manufacturers, and J. Williams cotton manufacturers – and of course, many will remember Bankfield Mill as being Parkinson's Factory, the pill makers. It burnt down in August 1977, in a spectacular blaze: only the walls and foundations now remain, and these will soon disappear if the new Oval Centre ever comes to fruition. The mill at the time of the fire was disused, but belonged to the metal merchant firm of Woodfield and Turner, who was in negotiation with the council over demolishing the building – the fire in effect saved them the job.

BANKFIELD SHED, BRUN STREET, BURNLEY

Bankfield Shed was a little further down Curzon Street than Bankfield Mill, nearer the town centre. The stone-built 'arches' at the bottom of Parker Street are relicts; all that survive from the mill. This is the oldest part of the Bankfield Mill complex, and is marked on the 1851 map. The mill was being run by Brun Street Manufacturing Co. Ltd in the 1920s, and a short time later during a depression in the cotton trade 564 looms were stopped. The mill never re-opened following a disastrous fire in March 1929, and was used for many years afterwards as a scrap yard.

Bankfield Shed. (courtesy of the Briercliffe Society)

Another view of Bankfield Shed. (courtesy of the Briercliffe Society)

Being brought up in this area, the latter was a prized and valued playground of childhood days. Some strange square wooden boxes mounted on a chassis could be turned around by a handle inside – I never did find out what they were originally used for!

BANKHOUSE MILL, ROYLE ROAD, BURNLEY

The cotton manufacturers and spinner Hopwood and Pollard were working the Bankhouse Mill in 1824. It is possible that this was another name for the Salford Mill. Nothing remains; the area has long since been redeveloped.

BARDEN MILL (ALSO KNOWN AS REEDLEY HALLOWS MILL), BARDEN LANE, BURNLEY

Worked by the Barden Mill Co. (Burnley) Ltd, in 1945, which was incorporated in 1912. Factory extensions were carried out in 1953–54 and, in 1960, the firm merged with Stott and Smith Ltd, of Manchester. The products were exported to Scandinavia, Canada, and the United States as well as Australia and New Zealand. The warehouse part of the mill that fronted on to Barden Lane had a cast-iron lintel with the date 1920. This part of the mill (now the car park) was demolished in 1997 when an opportunity arose by some quick thinking sales person, and they decided to have a 'demolition sale'. The rest of the mill, that which was the weaving shed, is now the Barden Mill Shop complex, which attracts shoppers and tourist from a wide area. In July 2007 a plan was put forward for a £1 million marina as part of the development and expansion of the Barden Mill complex, and approved in 2008.

BELLE VUE MILL, WESTGATE

Worked by Thomas Burrows Ltd, who also worked the Britannia Mill, both in 1923, and 1945. In 1905 it was resolved that the Thomas Burrows Co. should purchase from Mr William West, of No. 87 Gladstone Terrace, Harle Syke, the Belle Vue Mill, on Westgate Burnley, for the sum of £5,960. This amount was proportioned out as follows: £4,000 in respect of lands, buildings and premises, including fixtures, fixed machinery, and the sum of £1,960 in respect of the loose machinery and effects. The Belle Vue Mill was built in 1863 (see date plate on front elevation) as a cotton-weaving mill. The 1844–48 map shows a cotton mill a little further back towards the canal, and a square-shaped building where the present-day building stands today. An engine house here at Belle View Mill was demolished in 1980. The side elevation at the Mitre end of the building appears to indicate that this part, the warehouse section, was originally constructed with just the ground floor and first floor. Today the old mill is used by the CMA Tools, which was founded in 1968.

BISHOP HOUSE MILL, RYLANDS STREET, BURNLEY

Bishop House Mill was erected in 1886. The Bishop House Mill Co. Ltd was a room and power company in the 1920s, when W. Walton's and Son Ltd worked here. The mill was being worked

The rear side of Belle Vue Mill.

by William Bancroft and Co. (1932) Ltd, in 1945, and W. Smith and Son (Burnley) Ltd, along with Harry Walton and Sons Ltd who operated 868 looms. William Bancroft and Co. Ltd, were operating 124 looms at this time manufacturing shirting, twills and flannelettes. In more recent years the mill was occupied by 'Ultra Finishing' while the top or the Briercliffe Road end of the mill was worked until quite recently by 'Grenfell'. The mill lodge attached to the Bishop House Mill was the scene of a sad drowning accident involving a young lad aged just six years old in late July 1928. Young Harold Smith was playing with his friend near the lodge when he fell in. His young playmate quickly ran for help and told William Wilkinson, a joiner working nearby, what had happened. William rushed to the place and seeing nothing dived in. He soon found the young lad, but he was beyond help. Mill lodges were notorious places for drownings, particularly to the young who saw them as some sort of adventure playground. There was an even more serious incident at the Bishop House Mill in December 1948, when the flywheel which powered the 1,500 looms of the mill engine 'ran away'. In the devastation that followed Miss Selina Warburton was killed, and number of other weavers received injuries – there was also extensive damage done to the mill fabric. Near here at one time was a farm tenanted by Thomas Bishop, hence the name Bishop House – the farm consisted of just one acre. The farm or farm buildings shows up on the Ordinance Survey map of 1844–48. The mill including the weaving shed was demolished in 2007 for a new supermarket complex.

BLUTCHER STREET MILL

Blutcher Street is the old name for that part of St James's Street from the Boot Inn to Yorkshire Street near the Keirby roundabout, being named after a Prussian General who arrived at

Waterloo at a critical time. I have little information on the Blutcher Street Mill, other than it was worked by James Pickup in 1818–1820. Obviously nothing remains: this area of town was widened in 1864 due to increased traffic, and has been altered greatly ever since that time.

BRENNAND MILL

The mill was named after John Brennand, an overseer and cotton manufacturer in town and located on Brennand Street and Briercliffe Road, it was built some time before 1820. The mill was worked by Taylor and Clarkson Ltd in the mid-1920s, a firm incorporated in 1917, and John Wood and Son, in 1945. In 1975 the firm of Dorma took over the mill to produce pillowcases, and later in 1975 the Wigan-based development firm of Trinity Investments got planning permission to develop the site into what is now the Briercliffe Shopping Centre – however, a small portion of the mill still survives on Bracewell Street.

BRIDGE END MILL

This is probably the earliest documentation of Bridge End Mill. This is mentioned in a paper in Burnley reference library, and states that on 24 May 1736:

John Halstead of Bridge End in Habergham Eves surrendered to Henry Halstead, his son.
a. One cottage and one dyehouse adjoining and lately erected and standing on the northeast part of the ancient messuage called Bridge End.
b. A piece of land on the River Calder with the mill and building lately erected, being taken out of a close (enclosure) called Higher Holme belonging to Bridge End.
c. A piece of land on the opposite side of the Calder and adjoining the call (sluice) called by the name of The Hagg.

Bennett in his *History of Burnley* Vol. III gives us a little more information.

The Halsteads built 'a cloth mill and another dyehouse' on their land on the opposite bank of the river (Calder Street) and turned the old dyehouse into a fulling mill. In order to provide water to turn the waterwheel that was necessary to drive the machinery of the fulling mill, they 'erected a call [narrow wooden aqueduct] below the new dye house and mill and brought one other water called Brown [Brun] by a sate [narrow trench for running water]. In addition, in order to obtain more water for fulling and dyeing purposes, they constructed a weir across the Calder. The Halsteads of Bridge End and the Sagars of Coal Clough quarrelled about the new buildings in the present Calder Street. It was alleged that the new mill and the new dyehouse were partly erected on 'Sagar land', that the goyt passed through Sagar's field, and that one end of the new weir was on Sagar's property. It was further stated that the Halsteads had cut down trees growing on Sagar's land and had used the timber in the erection of the mill and had also taken 'great stones' from Sagar's property. One of the trees that was cut down was an elder 'so large that it would make coffin boards for a man'. The increased volume of water at one point in the river, created by the weir, endangered the banks, but when Sagar sent 'three or four workmen for twenty or thirty days together to support his banks with great quantities of wood and one or two workmen stood up in the middle of the water to drive piles down', instead of assisting the workmen Halstead forced up the water and 'milled at night' [as well as by day]. Then Sagar sent his nephew to cut down the weir, but Halstead and two of his servants 'cut his thumb half-off and put it out of joint' and threatened to shoot him as he passed by Bridge End House. Halstead was forced by the authorities to stop the goyt through Sagar's field and therefore in 1740 he leased another 'piece of land at the back of two dwelling houses belonging to William Holt, apothecary, to drive a sough or sate through the said land to carry the water from the Brown into the Calder in order to better the supply of water to the fulling mill or walk mill of Henry Halstead.' These buildings in Calder Vale Road and Calder Street housed one of Burnley's earliest enterprises in textile manufacture on a large scale.

The 'cloth mill' contained a number of handlooms and the existence of a fulling mill suggests that it was a woollen cloth that was made; a separate building for dyeing implies some specialisation. The 'Tenter Fields' shown on an old map as being near Orchard Bridge were used as drying and stretching grounds after the fulling process; the spinning was probably done by women and children in their own homes. There are no records to tell us whether any other factories existed in Burnley at such an early date. The Sagars of Coal Clough 1660–1740 had 'a shop' but that may have been only a small shed used for weaving. We do know that the Bridge End Mill was worked by James Sutcliffe 'cotton spinner and sizer' in 1843, and was sold to Charles Waddington for £4,500 in 1871.

BRIDGE STREET MILL

Nothing remains. This mill, obviously on Bridge Street, stood directly across from the bottom of Manchester Road, and dated from around 1851 (when it shows up on a map for that year) and survived in connection with the cotton trade to around the mid-1870s. This may have been Harrison and Ashworth's spinning mill, noted on Bridge Street in the year 1865: the following evidence supports this. The Bridge Street Mill was offered for sale by auction on 28 July 1877, and was described as follows:

All those valuable premises formerly used as a cotton mill by the late Richard Harrison, situated on Bridge Street and Howe Street (late Nile Street) known as 'Bridge Street Mill'. It consists of fireproof cotton mill four storeys high, one three-storey warehouse, boiler house, engine house, chimney and other erections, together with the engine water cistern etc. A portion of the premises are occupied by John Taylor and John Nuttall. The site of Lot One contains 673 square yards of land and is free from ground rent. The property being situated near the Market Hall forms very eligible for adapting into shops, warehouses etc.

The *Burnley Gazette* on 3 March 1856 gave a report of a fire on Bridge Street:

About ten minutes past six o'clock on Friday morning, a fire broke out at the Old Mill, at the bottom of Bridge Street, belonging to Mr H.D. Fielding. In a short time the flames increased rapidly in the first and second storeys, facing Water Street. The town's hose was quickly on the spot, the greatest exertions were used, and the fire was completely subdued about half past seven o'clock. A portion of the card-room floor fell in, the floor above was also much burned. Much valuable machinery was destroyed, and the rest is greatly damaged. The cotton of the scutching room is destroyed, the damage is estimated upwards of £1,000. The machinery is insured in the West of England Office, and the building with the Leeds and Yorkshire. It is said that the fire broke out in the card-room. A fire broke out in this mill on the 14th. December last, exactly ten weeks ago, when considerable damage was done to the cotton and machinery.

The mill was on the left-hand side of Bridge Street, just beyond Fleet Street and the old Sun Inn. Researching mills in this area of town, and the old Wapping District, can be frustrating to say the least. For instance, John Eltoft was working a cotton-manufacturing mill in Bridge Street in 1818–1820. In the same period William Dale worked a cotton manufacture and spinning mill on Bridge Street, and The Bridge Street Mill Co. was at No. 28 Bridge Street in 1923; they were cotton-waste dealers.

BRIERCLIFFE MILL, HARLE SYKE

Briercliffe Mill was worked by South View Manufacturing Co. Ltd in 1945, and in 1962, and at the former date the mill was running 484 looms and William Taylor of No. 3 Burnley Road Briercliffe was the secretary and salesman at the mill. This mill started as a 'room and power company' under the title of the Briercliffe Mill Co. in 1880. Among the other cotton manufacturers here were the Altham family when it was known as 'Tay Hoyle'. Abraham Altham of course was also a tea merchant and the founder of the still surviving 'Altham's Travels' firm. The mill survives today, but is used for other purposes.

BRISTOL MILL, CALDERVALE ROAD, BURNLEY

Bristol Mill was worked by the Hollingreave Manufacturing Co. Ltd in 1923, who also worked the Clifton Mill on Ashfield Road. The mill formerly occupied the land now taken as car parking on the right-hand side of Caldervale Road, before the former Paper Mill.

Nothing remains of the actual mill, save for the retaining wall facing the river. The Bristol Mill contained a site area of 1,996 square yards and had a 999-year lease taken out in June 1907 from Burnley Paper Works to the Hollingreave Manufacturing Co. It was a single-storey brick-built building, with an engine house at the Paper Mill end. In here was a boiler, built by Yates and Thom, which was 24ft long and 7½ft wide. This supplied the steam to a 75hp horizontal tandem compound-surface condensing engine with 7in and 14in cylinders, with an 18in stroke. In 1949, the shuttle manufacturing firm of Thomas Comstive Ltd celebrated 100 years in business at the Bristol Mill. Thomas Comstive, the founder of the business, lived at Sefton Terrace, Burnley with his wife Elizabeth and four sons and two daughters. Thomas died in 1886, but his sons carried on the business. His son William died from blood poisoning in 1933. William was buried at Haggate Chapel.

BRITANNIA MILL

The Britannia Mill worked as a weaving shed and operated from 1911 through to 1996. Thomas Burrows worked both the Britannia Mill and the Belle Vue Mill on Westgate in the 1920s as a cotton manufacturer. This mill was one of the most modern mills in Burnley, and here 1,088 looms were installed. It was due to the foresight of William Henry Burrows that when the mill was affected with mining subsidence in later years, there were not more serious repercussions. This was due to the chimney: before the construction of the mill chimney he ordered that the foundations to the chimney be doubled. The mill survives, the main elevation being on Rylands Street up Colne Road as a red-brick weaving shed. The mill is now worked by Robert McBride. In October 1955 a meeting was held by the 200 operatives at the Britannia Mill who were thrown out of work by subsidence, probably caused by mining at the Bank Hall Colliery on Colne Road: this marked the end of textiles at Britannia Mill. Consultants had previously advised the firm to have the top 12ft of the mill chimney removed in March 1954, which reduced the height of the chimney to 128ft. The firm ceased production on Friday 30 September 1955. At the time the mill stopped, it was one of the few mills in Burnley that was working full-time. In June 1957, the mayor of Burnley Mrs M.A. Battle reopened the mill as part of Burnley Aircraft Products Ltd. The BAP commenced operations at Fulledge in 1938, after the Fulledge Mill had been acquired by the Corporation to provide alternative employment to textiles in the town. In February 1993, there was a suspicious blaze at Robert McBride's factory when damage to the value of £2 million was caused.

BROWHEAD MILL, BROWHEAD ROAD, BURNLEY

The Browhead Mill was being worked by Mark Kippax and Sons Ltd in 1945, who were operating 1,013 looms. They had reopened the premises in July 1934; the year before the Browhead Mill was worked by the Exors of J. West, but all the looms at this time were stopped. Mark Kippax and Sons had transferred from the Brownside and Marlfield Sheds to move here. The Browhead Mill was built from May 1906, and started in February 1907, and went on to contain over 1,000 looms. The mill was built as a weaving shed, with warehouse and engine room to the front elevation. The engine here was a cross compound of 500hp with 17in high-pressure cylinders and 35in low-pressure cylinders. The piston had a 4ft stroke and ran at a speed of 70rpm. The engine flywheel was 15ft in diameter, grooved for fifteen ropes. Two Lancashire boilers supplied steam to the engine. The Browhead Mill was run by John West, who also ran the Rake Head Mill. John West, was a relation of William West of Simpson and West, and also a partner in that firm and ran mills in Briercliffe, and the Belle Vue and Spring Garden Mills at Burnley. John died in 1901, but the Browhead continued for a number of years under the title of the Exors of John West. There is a West Street close by which recalls the family. This (Browhead Mill) is the mill taken over in later years by Skippers Garages, when they moved from Caldervale, it still remains, but the warehouse has been demolished, including the fine engine house and the rest greatly altered, although the weaving shed section remains for car body and mechanical repairs.

BROWN STREET MILL, BROWN STREET, BURNLEY

The firm of Tattersall and Cross operated this mill in 1824; although it dated from slightly earlier, it also went under the name of 'Tattersall and Slater' at one time. Later it was being worked, in 1868, by John Brennand, who gave his name to Brennand Street, and who lived at Byerden House. John also worked the Rake Head Mill at this time. John Brennand and Brothers were working the Rake Head Mill as far back as 1848. The Brown Street Mill was offered for sale by auction in the *Burnley Advertiser* on 2 October 1875. It was then situated in Brown Street, Gas Street and Veevers Street, and 'formerly in the occupation of John Brennand'. This implies that the mill was then on the site of, or even the same building now occupied by, Stanworth's Engineering. It consisted of three lofty rooms, fourteen yards by thirteen yards each, three rooms seventeen yards by five yards each, and three rooms twenty-one yards by eight yards each. The steam engine here was a McNaughted beam engine of 25hp, with 21in and 20in cylinders, 4ft stroke, flywheel 14ft 6in in diameter with solid ashlar foundation. The boiler was 18ft 6in by 6ft 2in with a single flue. Gas was used to illuminate a factory in Brown Street, which might have been the Brown Street Mill. It may be that the present-day shops on Brown Street have been converted from an old mill, but not the one related to above. Certainly this was the site of a mill which shows up on the map of 1851. The stone troughing on these shops also indicate a building pre-1860s. Brown Street Mill was stopped eventually by outdated machinery and lack of space, meaning it was unable to compete with the large and more efficient mills that were becoming the norm at this time.

BULL CROFT MILL

We learn of the Bull Croft Mill in Bennett's *History of Burnley* Vol. III, in which he says:

> In 1770, we hear of a fulling mill on the Bull Croft; the goyt from the Calder which turned that mill was also used for turning the waterwheel used for the drainage system of the nearby coal mine.

Bull Croft was the area around Hargreaves Street today, and Coal Street recalls the old coal mine mentioned above. It appears that the mill, and indeed the coal pit, which at one time was worked by a member of the Grimshaw family of Pendleside, and who gave their name to Grimshaw Street, had ceased to exist by the year 1827.

BURNLEY WOOD MILL, OXFORD ROAD, BURNLEY

Burnley Wood Mill was built as a weaving shed in around 1850 with a floor space of 3,870 yards and a second floor warehouse with 684 yards of floor space. The sheds were built of stone with slate roof, and it drew its water for the boiler from the River Calder. Burnley Wood Mill still survives, being the large mill on the corner of Oxford Road and Parliament Street, (the last mill on the left going up Oxford Road towards Todmorden Road), and is now used by a firm making floor laminates. The Burnley Wood Mill was said to have been 'stopped' along with its 926 looms when worked by Collinge Brothers in 1934. The report also went on to say that the mill was now being taken over by a firm of printers. This would have been Veevers and Hensman Ltd printers. In 1865 the Burnley Wood Mill was being worked by Henry and Edmund Rawlinson.

BYERDEN MILL, COLNE ROAD, BURNLEY

The mill dated from around the late 1870s, and in 1879 was being worked by Barker and Hartley, cotton manufacturers. Richard Stuttard Ltd worked this mill from at least the mid-1920s through to 1945 and beyond, and also worked the nearby Primrose Mill. This firm was working 2,709 looms in 1940. Richard was of Pendle Forest stock, came from Wheatley Lane and described himself as a 'cotton manufacturer' in the 1880s when he was living on Allen Street off Colne Road. It was around 1845 that Richard Stuttard left Wheatley Lane and came to Burnley, where he went into business as a clogger on Colne Road. Richard married Catherine

Burnley Wood Mill.

Hind, the daughter of Shuttleworth Hind of the Sparrow Hawk Hotel at Burnley in 1861 at St Peter's church in Burnley. Out of his wages earned as a clogger Richard put money to one side and eventually was able to purchase a few looms at Byerden Mill when it was being run by Mr Halstead. Richard prospered through hard work, and by around 1883 was able to purchase the whole of Byerden Mill. Later the concern became a limited company, worked under the title of Richard Stuttard Ltd. At the time of Richard's death in December 1895 the mill was employing over 300 hands and contained 1,010 looms. Richard Stuttard was a great supporter of the then new St Andrew's Club near Duke Bar, which in recent years has closed down; he also worshiped at St Andrew's church close by. Richard was buried in a family vault at St James' church at Briercliffe. The memorial is not hard to miss, being the largest structure nearest the Queen Street Mill corner. Like Richard, it appears many other local manufacturers tried in vain to gain immortality with their huge monuments to their existence. There were at least three mills named Byerden in this area at various times. One of these today is occupied by a builder's merchant directly across from Pratt Street on Colne Road. Part of the former mill weaving shed is used by them as warehousing, and the surrounding mill wall survives, or at least did until quite recently, on Colne Road itself.

CALDERVALE MILL, CALDERVALE ROAD, BURNLEY

Caldervale Mill was worked by F. Parkinson and Co. in 1923, who also worked the Ashfield Mill. The fine, but derelict, engine house and chimney still survive at Caldervale Mills, and the Ashfield Road side of the mill. The premises were bought by C.G. Skippers in March 1959, who announced plans to convert the old mill into garage premises at a cost of £75,000. In November 1961, a ferocious blaze swept through the mill, gutting it and causing £30,000 worth of damage. In more recent times the site of most of Ashfield Mill was used as a lorry park for the now former Burnley Paper Works. Part of the walls to Ashfield Shed remains at the lower end near the engine house, and has a fine arch. The engine-house has two large arch windows on the gable, and three on the side elevation, all of dressed stone, with a random rubble building at the rear. The round chimney is also built of dressed stone, and has a tree growing out of the top! It appears that there has been a recent planning application to convert the former engine house into offices, in 2001. It was here in 1887 that Thomas Burrows commenced business on his own account in Calder Vale, he later took over the Belle Vue Mill, and later the firm also erected the Britannia Mill at Queensgate.

CAIRO MILL, PICKLES STREET, WHITTLEFIELD

This was worked by Robert Pickles Ltd (hence the name of Pickle Street). The mill, built in 1886, a date borne by a cast lintel over a loading door, has now been demolished. The firm of Robert Pickles was one of the largest textile firms in the entire country, with five mills in Burnley, one at Todmorden, and one at Padiham. Robert Pickles was born in 1816, had a 'smattering' of education at Roughlee and his first mill was that at Barley Green in the shadow of Pendle Hill at Barley Village. Barley Green House was the residence of a number of manufacturers at various times. It was a sort of 'halfway' stage between the cottage industry and the power mills: a dandy shop occupied the upper floors with dandy looms for cotton cloth. Also here was an upper-floor doorway for passing out the bundles of cloth and weft. Later, a power mill was constructed, now on the site of the Water Board's filter house; water coming from Ogden Brook over the road in troughs powered the water wheel. Later a steam engine was introduced, but a powerful flood in 1881 caused £2,000 worth of damage to the old mill, and probably spelt its end.

In 1888 the mill was bought by Nelson Corporation for the water rights and the beginnings of the Ogden Reservoir. Robert Pickles was a keen inventor, it was he who invented the 'check strap' which was modified and was still in use even in the latter days of King Cotton. In the early days it was not uncommon for Robert to set off walking to Manchester once a month to sell his wares. Robert died in 1892, and was succeeded by his son, Thomas, and his two grandsons. As late as the 1950s, the managing director, Thomas Pickles, and another director, Charles Francis were the great-grandsons of the founder, Robert Pickles, keeping up the family ties with the business. In May 1900 William Dean, aged twenty, who was employed at the mill, was killed through being taken around the belt shafting. George Nadin, the great-great-uncle of the writer, gave evidence at the inquest that followed – the inquest gave graphic details, with little regard, it seems, at the time for close relations to the deceased. 'Part of the deceased's body was on the shafting, and the other part on the cropping machine. The legs were torn off the body', it was stated. A serious fire at Cairo Mill in April 1945 caused £10,000 worth of damage.

CALDER STREET MILL

A mill on Calder Street off St James's Street that existed from 1833, through to around 1910. James Pollard was working a mill on Calder Street in the late 1840s. Not to be confused with the Cheapside Mill or indeed Cuckoo Mill which also went by this name.

Caldervale Shed, Caldervale Road/Ashfield Road, Burnley.

This was worked as part of the Caldervale Mills, where the weaving was carried out, and Robert Emmott and Son were operating here in 1879. The mills at this time employed 145 men and women – Robert himself lived at No. 29 Caldervale Road. The Caldervale Sheds were worked by William Brierley Ltd in 1923. During a depression in the cotton trade from around the 1920s, there were 516 looms stopped at Brierley's. Little remains of the mill today.

Caledonia Mill, Sandygate, Burnley.

The original Caledonia Mill was built beside the Leeds and Liverpool Canal as a small cotton mill around 1850, which shows up on the 1851 map. The mill may have been destroyed by a fire, but remains of the original mill walls can still be seen besides the canal. Next door to this was the Caledonia gasometer and boiler works, which had been in existence from around 1835. The boiler works was eventually taken over by the mill, which extended across both sites from about 1860, when purchased by the Grimshaw Brothers. They are listed in 1868 as working the mill. Further expansion took place around the mid-1870s, when the mill was bought by Whitaker and Lupton. Whitaker and Co. (Burnley) Ltd, cotton-waste spinners, were working the mill in the 1920s. In March 1929, a serious fire caused £5,000 worth of damage. The fire, accompanied by a slump in trade, meant that the Caledonia Mill in 1934 (including its 186 dobbie and shoddy looms) was 'stopped'. In 1935, the mill consisted of three floors with a floor space of 1,110 yards, and had a sale price of £800. By the mid-1940s, however, Morris and Son (Textile Machinists) Ltd were running the Caledonia Mill. The mill was closed down in 1982, and at a later date, bought by the council, who demolished the weaving shed to provide better access to a number of small units in the rest of the mill. Today, these units are let out to small firms and businesses, and the site of the weaving shed is now car-parking space. The Caledonian Mill was up for sale by auction in 1871 and included 'ten carding engines, 36 inches on the wire'.

Cameron Mill, Howsin Street, Burnley

This mill dated from 1906 and was installed with nearly 1,000 looms; it finished weaving around 1969. The Cameron Mill still survives and until quite recently was given a new lease of life by being worked by PenDelfin. This and the Livingstone Mill, were being worked by John Grey Ltd (1893) in 1945 operating 2,289 looms. John Grey, later Sir John Grey, was born in Fulledge in 1875 and was one of Burnley's leading industrialists. He received his knighthood in 1935 for services and leadership to the Lancashire cotton trade. Cameron Mill was closed down during the war, but reopened in 1946 when both this and the Livingstone Mill were re-spaced to meet the modern methods of weaving and health and safety at that time. In 1948 the firm became a limited company, and in the same year absorbed the firm of Thomas Fletcher and Sons Ltd of Nelson, makers of sateens, poplins, rayon and broad lining clothes. The chairman of the new company was Sir John Haworth Grey, who had been knighted in 1935 for his services to the cotton industry. Sir John Haworth Grey used to live at the large 'Thornleigh' house at No. 317 Colne Road – he died in 1960 and was succeeded by James Michael Harling Grey. Around the late 1950s the firm was able to open new offices at

Cameron Mill.

Manchester, the old one having lasted over seventy years, and were able to purchase the King's Mill in Burnley. The Cameron mill today is composed of a single storey red-bricked weaving mill with two-storey office warehouse accommodation with sandstone quoins. An interesting boiler/engine house can be seen at the bottom of Birkbeck Way. The famous firm of Pendelfin had been at Cameron Mill for around fifteen years, when in June 1986 the two-storey section at the bottom of Howsin Street was gutted by fire. The firm did however recover, until it closed down permanently in March 2006 (with the loss of fourteen jobs) due to competition from the Far East. A long-serving employee at Cameron Mill was Wilfred Hartley, who retired in 1953, with his son Fred: they completed 100 years of service to the firm. Wilfred began his working life aged ten years old at Livingstone Mill, which at that time was just four years old. He began to learn to weave, and then went on to 'tenting' for the other weavers. When Cameron Mill opened Wilfred was transferred there. Only once in sixty years was he ever late for work. On that occasion he was met at the mill gate by the manager who remarked, 'this is a bit unusual, Wilfred'.

'Aye', said Wilfred, 'I have been up all night with my son who has whooping cough.'

'That'll do then', said the manager, 'We'll say no more about it.'

CANAL STREET MILL, CANAL STREET, BURNLEY

This is the mill facing you as you go up Canal Street, besides the Newtown Steel Works, and occupies the top right-hand corner and the blank wall of the mill to the left. It was worked by John Jackson and Co. in 1923 and 1945; he operated 424 loom at the latter date manufacturing twills and jeanettes. The mill dates from around 1890, and was the scene of a terrible fire in October 1904. Two men perished in the fire; James Marsh was a twister at the mill, and the other was Walter Jackson, son of the lessee of the mill. The mill, which is in the form of a letter L, belonged originally to the Burnley Iron Works who leased out the premise to Messrs Jackson and Co. and the George Street Manufacturing Co. who between them ran nearly 1,000, looms. The mill consisted of three floors, one below ground for some distance at the back end of the mill, but above ground nearer the front of the building, which was used for storing yarn. On the second floor was warehouse accommodation with offices at the far end. Above this was the winding and beaming machinery, and an attic used for taping and twisting. The fire was caused when young Walter Jackson tried to light a gas burner and an explosion ensued, lighting a number of healds. Although much damage was done to the mill, and two lives were lost, it did survive and is still with us. The mill boasted having one of the oldest winders in Lancashire in 1937 by way of Ellen Thorp. 'Old Ellen', as the workers called her, of Duerden Street, was seventy-seven years old, and still working at the mill. Ellen was Yorkshire-born, at Gargrave, and started at a mill there as a child. Later she went into service at Bolton Woods near Bolton Abbey, and after a period of 'retirement' at Shipley she came to Burnley about 1885 and earned a living working at the various sheds for sick weavers. In 1917 she started as a winder at the Canal Street Mill where she was one of the liveliest employees in the shed.

CAPE TOWN MILL, TUNNEL STREET, BURNLEY

The Cape Town Mill was one of Robert Pickles Ltd. The mill still survives, down at Whittlefield, although it has been extensively modified, with steel sheeting on top of original walls. This might suggest that there had been a fire at the mill at some time. At the Tunnel Street end of the mill are the only remains of the original mill walls. Both the Cape Town Mill and the Cairo Mill are named after the places where Robert Pickles exported his cotton to. Robert Pickles was working this mill until 1945, and in the 1880s he employed 160 hands at his mills.

CENTRAL MILL, ALBERT STREET, BURNLEY

The mill dates from around 1888. It was worked by Edward Houlding in 1923, who a few years later had 484 looms 'stopped' as the depression in the trade took hold. Later, from around 1930, a firm of cabinet makers named Earnshaw Brothers and Booth took over the Central Mill. Albert Street is off Yorkshire Street, and the mill was on the left-hand side.

CHARLOTTE STREET MILL, CHARLOTTE STREET, BURNLEY

This mill was formerly known as Queen Street Mill, and dated from the late 1840s. Following a fire in 1916, the mill was restored and renamed Charlotte Street Mill. A fine cast lintel here bears the date 1882. The mill has been extensively renovated in the past few years, and is now used by small industrial units. The two end parts are the oldest, the middle bit, strangely enough, being built last.

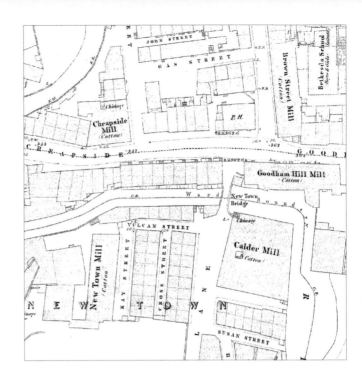

Cheapside Mill map of 1851.

CHEAPSIDE MILL

No longer with us, the Cheapside mill operated from around 1816 to around 1860. Cheapside is the old name for the middle portion from Cow Lane to the Cross Keys end of St James's Street. The Cheapside Mill was on the corner of Calder Street on the Westgate side and St James's Street. The mill, also known as 'Howarth's Factory', was built around 1816 as a cotton-spinning mill and had a capacity of some 20,000 to 30,000 spindles, but finished around the 1860s. Around 1865 the mill was taken over by John Gott, a waste dealer, for a short period, and the mill later remained empty for a while. After John Gott finished with the mill, the engine house was used as a smithy and a nail-making shop. James Rawlinson then took on the old mill and used it as a leather works and warehouse, later trading as Rawlinson and Holden until around 1880, when a fire destroyed a considerable portion of the premises. The mill was originally three storeys in height and fronted onto St James's Street and on Calder Street went as far as the Pack Horse Inn, later the Christian Science establishment, and now the Concert Artists' Club. Around 1871, the owner Mrs Howarth converted the portion of the mill that abutted St James's Street into five single-storey lock-up shops. By the 1890s, these were occupied by Councillor Harker, Mr Bromley, Mr Whittaker, Mr Boys and Peter Grant, a clogger who had his premises on Calder Street. On a cold winters day in January 1896 the base of the old mill chimney gave way and it came crashing down, destroying the shops and taking away the lives of former cricketer Richard Boys and his wife. In the debris was also found the body of a young twelve-year-old named Margaret McClusky, who'd been sitting waiting patiently on a bench in Peter Grant's clogger's shop for her fathers' shoes, which were being mended. Fears had been expressed over the old mill chimney for years, and large portions often dropped off the structure at the rear of the shops. The chimney was reduced in height a short time before the accident – but to no avail. How the accident happened, we will now never know, but one theory put forward was that it was caused by rats! Scores of these were often seen at the back of the old mill, and it was thought that they burrowed under the foundations of the chimney, causing it to fall. On one occasion it was stated that a 'regiment' of rats were seen near the river. Following the accident the buildings on St James's Street were rebuilt and remain as we know them today – look for the date stone '1897' on the corner shop which recalls this. At the time of the accident the owner of the property was Mrs Dale, of Stoneyholme Cottage, the daughter of Mrs Anne Howarth, the original owner. The rest of the old mill was pulled down some time after – and the fatal and sad accident fell away into history. A red-bricked building attached to the rear of the former Pack Horse Inn on Calder Street appears to have been at one time warehouse accommodation. Notice the wooden hoist attachment above one of the doorways here.

CLIFTON MILL, ASHFIELD ROAD, BURNLEY

This mill no longer survives, save for a few boundary walls. The mill was on about a hundred yards down Ashfield Road from the Westgate, on the right-hand side, the site in later years being used as storage for the former Burnley Paper Mill trailers. Interestingly, a few cobble roads remain in this area, from the streets of housing that once occupied this district. The Collinge Brothers, cotton manufacturers, worked the Clifton Mill in 1879, although the mill itself dated from around 1865. It was also worked by the Hollingreave Manufacturing Co. Ltd in 1923, who also worked the Bristol Mill on Caldervale Road. The latter firm had nearly 900 looms 'stopped' through a depression in trade during the 1930s. Alright Products Ltd worked at what was called the 'Clifton Works' in 1945.

CLOCK TOWER MILL, SANDYGATE, BURNLEY

Much has been written about George Slater; 'he who built the great mill on Sandygate, and then added a clock for pride'. I will therefore go briefly through his life, and his mills. George was born at Barnoldswick, in 1807, the son of William Slater, who had come to Burnley to work on the new canal. He entered into the town's staple industry by becoming a partner in the firm of Tattersall and Slater, whose premises were on Brown Street. George actually lived in Brown Street at this time, but soon moved, as he prospered, to Crow Nest at the bottom of Westgate. In later years he moved with his family to Whittlefield House, which many will remember as later being the Ponderosa Club. The house was demolished around 1976, for the new motorway. George decided to set up in manufacturing on his own account in a mill on Sandygate, the oldest part of what was to become Clock Tower Mill around 1840. This is the portion of the mill that runs at right angles to the canal and was used for mule spinning. It still survives, albeit in a dilapidated state. The 'New Mill' was added shortly after, that part running alongside the canal, with a weaving shed nearest the Canal Bridge. The 1851 census tells us that at this time George employed over 300 workers. Eight years later, the 'New Mill No. 2' was built further down the hill on Sandygate. Another mill across the way, also owned by George Slater, was connected with an overhead gangway built across the road. A serious fire gutted most of the mill in 1859: mills were notorious fire hazards, with oil-soaked floors

A view of Burnley, taken from Clock Tower Mill.

and cotton fluff covering everything in sight. Within two years the mill was rebuilt, and it was at this time that the clock which gave the mill its name was added. The clock was first set going in August 1863.

These must have been difficult times, not only for George, but for all manufacturers: it was the very height of the Cotton Famine. George, with other manufacturers, chartered ships to run the blockades of the American cotton ports, and they survived while many others succumbed to bankruptcy. Through these endeavours, George went on to become one of the town's greatest industrialists. It was George Slater who employed James Wiseman to build Slater Terrace in the 1840s, possibly unique worker's housing and mill premises combined. The terrace was last inhabited around 1900, and sporadic attempts to revitalise the property continue from time to time. The Sandygate Mill above the canal and Slater Terrace was also built by George Slater, and opened in 1862. In spite of all his wealth, George was not well liked; he would still arrive at the mill every morning at 6.00 a.m. and any factory worker coming after this time was turned away. George died at Whittlefield House in March 1873. When young George Slater, the eldest surviving son of George, got wed in 1864, a great celebration reception was held at Clock Tower Mill. Unlike other manufacturers, the Slater's contributed little to the town by way of open spaces and other amenities, such as those donated by William Thompson, and the Thornber's. However, we might include Slater Homes at Lane Head, donated by Col. Hubert Slater, following his death in 1911. A condition of the bequest was that the homes should not be used until the death of his sister, Emma. 'Dame' Emma, as she was sometimes known, died at Whittlefield House in February 1924, the last direct descendant of the Slater family. The Slater homes were opened in October 1927.

A disastrous fire destroyed the Clock Tower Mill in 1987, and it now lies a 'blackened ruin' much as the 'Pencilling Mill' did a century and more ago. John Watts (Burnley) Ltd, cotton-waste merchants, worked the Clock Tower Mill in later years. In 1843 the Canal Co. began to supply water to the mills, thus many of the canalside mills can be dated from this era. Bibby and Baron's, Finsley Mill (J. and G. Holgate), J. Greenwood and Sons, Rishton Mill and Hill Top Mill, Winterbottom's Corn Mill off Yorkshire Street, Oak Mount Mill (Hopwood's), Albion Mill in Finsley Gate, Walker Hey in the Meadows, Slater's, and Laws all began to draw water from the Canal in that year. There was a terrible accident at what was called 'Slater's factory' in April 1859 involving a forty-two-year-old woman named Susan Emmett. Mary Preston related that Susan had gone for some creels, and in doing so had to pass a vertical moving engine shaft. Her dress caught in the shafting and she was dragged to her death. The inquest was held at the former Neptune Inn across from the mill – a building that still survives, where the usual verdict was returned, that of 'accidental death'.

CORONATION MILL, ABINGER STREET, BURNLEY

Coronation Mill was worked by Harry Walton and Sons, in 1914, and the Fern Hill Manufacturing Co. Ltd in 1923, in premises also shared with the George Street Manufacturing Co. Ltd. The latter firm had 1,690 looms in operation at the beginning of the Second World War manufacturing warp, satteens, twills, cashmeres, drill, matting and handkerchief cloth. Twenty years later, only the George Street Manufacturing Co. Ltd was here. The mill was a red-brick weaving establishment and dated from 1911 – one of the last mills to be built in Burnley.

COW LANE MILL, HAMMERTON STREET, BURNLEY

Although named Cow Lane Mill, this mill was actually on Hammerton Street, and was later part of 'Proctor's Ironworks'. The part nearest the river, with the chimney, is now a nightclub, and is marked as Cow Lane Mill in 1851. It was also known as Rawlinson's Mill, or even Hammerton Street Mill, and was worked as a spinning mill. Samuel Smallpage was working the Hammerton Street Mill in 1848; Baldwin and Broxup in 1865, and Alexander Baldwin in 1879. The mill was put up for sale on 28 July 1877, and was described thus:

> That valuable stone built four storey cotton mill situated in Hammerton Street, Burnley called 'Cow Lane Mill' now in the occupation of Alexander Baldwin, as tenant together with the fire proof loom shed capable of containing 135 looms with spinning room there under and warping room over. Also the engine house, boiler house, fire proof scutching room, three storey high, chimney, office, warehouse and other erections. Together with a McNaughted beam engine of 30 horse power, boiler, shafting, gearing, gas and steam piping throughout.

CROFT STREET MILL, CROFT STREET, BURNLEY

Spencer and Moore were working a mill of this name at No. 5 Croft Street in the 1840s, although the mill dates from around 1820. There are no remains, although Croft Street still exists besides the bus station, for the site has been redeveloped beyond recognition.

CUCKOO MILL

Cuckoo Mill, on Blackburn Street, is probably Burnley's oldest surviving mill in its original form, and was initially a cotton-spinning mill, it was also known as 'Calder Street Mill'. A brewer named John Hargreaves first built the mill in 1833, and it was run by a vertical engine, with beams connecting rods and drums, all of which were made of timber. The mill's location besides the River Calder was deliberate – the water being drawn off to feed the boilers of the engine. Cuckoo Mill was closed down during the Cotton Famine of 1862–64, failing through outdated machinery and the effects of the famine itself. Cuckoo Mill is built four storeys high, with four loading bay windows on the left, and two on the right. On the gable end wall at the Royle Road end of the building can be seen the height of the former buildings that used to run up the rest of Blackburn Street, the houses of Robert Varley and Ambrose Wilson in the 1920s. The area behind the main mill used now as the scrap yard was the Royle Foundry, a brass works. But John Crook built a spinning mill here along with a foundry about 1800. The mill was later used as a weaving shed, a bakery and then the foundry. Look also for the stable accommodation on the river-side of the building, and the middle wooden bar evidently chewed away by a restless horse. For many years from the late 1890s the mill was under Stephen Murphy and run as a marine store. By the 1920s, the mill had been taken over by Wallace Reader, and again used as a marine store, and it continues under the same name to this day.

DANDY SHOP, KEIGHLEY GREEN, BURNLEY

A 'dandy shop' was a mill or factory where handlooms were put to use. 'Some few attempts were made to introduce handlooms into buildings by the factory system, as was done by Messrs Spencer and Moore in what was long known as the 'dandy shop' in Keighley Green, but without a great measure of success', we are told in Kneeshaw's *Burnley in the Nineteenth Century*. The dandy shop has obviously long gone, but it may have been on the site of the later Parsonage Mill, its address being Massey Street. The Dandy Shop, also known as 'Bazing Hall', was built in 1787 and contained handlooms for woollen weaving. It closed down around 1825. 'The dandy shop or "Bazing Hall" in 1824, was the mill in Massey Street that was bought by Lord Massey and his two sons, hence the name of the street which still survives. Tradition says that they washed the wool in the River Brun, and employed three sorters.'

DANESHOUSE MILL, ELM STREET, BURNLEY

The Daneshouse Mill Co. were working the Daneshouse Mill in 1868 and 1879, and B. Thornber and Sons (1931) Ltd worked it in 1945, running 17,396 ring spindles. The Thornber family was one of Burnley's leading industrialist concerns, and ran several mills in the town. Benjamin Thornber, the founder, was born in 1800 at Cote Farm in Gisburn. He came to Burnley with all his worldly processions on a handcart, to start a new life with his family in 1851.

He found work as a weaver at Hopwood's Oak Mount Mill, and in 1856 began in partnership with one of his wife's relations, Caleb Duckworth, with power looms at the old Heasandford corn mill. The 'powered' looms were actually water fed from millponds. The old Heasandford Mill, or 'Pheasant Ford Mill' as it is spelt on the map of 1851, appears to have been much nearer to the present Bank Hall Park, roughly where the monument to the mining industry is today. Soon afterwards they rented seventy-two looms at the Market Bridge Mill, which was on River Street, near Hammerton Street. They progressed further, moving into the Trafalgar Mill in 1858, but the partnership was dissolved soon after this, Caleb preferring to enter the grocery business. Benjamin struck out on his own account, and took into partnership three of his younger sons – a previous partnership with the two eldest had come to grief. They had survived the great distress caused by the Cotton Famine, and, in 1874, they moved to Healey Wood Shed, and in 1875, Daneshouse Mill. The Healey Wood Mill was given up altogether in 1881, and Throstle Mill next door to Daneshouse Mill was acquired. Benjamin died in 1885, and at the time the firm was running 1,420 looms and 44,000 spindles – one of the largest cotton manufacturing concerns in Burnley. The old gentleman was taken back to whence he came and was buried at Gisburn Churchyard. On the day of his funeral crowds gathered and carriages stretched back over Coldweather Hill with folks wishing to pay their last respects to a grand old gentleman and employer.

Old Hall Mill, a short distance away from Daneshouse Mill, was also acquired by the Thornber's. The Daneshouse Mill was totally wiped out in a £1 million blaze in June 1996; the site is now a car park and small modern and unattractive 'tin' industrial units. Many of the mill hands and workers took their work really seriously – it was more a way of life than a means of earning a living to many: take John Emmott of No. 26 Haydock Street, who completed over sixty-six years service with Messrs Thornber at their Daneshouse Mills by the time he retired in January 1949. John started at the mill when aged just ten and a half years as a part-timer, learning to 'reach in' for 3s 3d a week. He started on his own twisting frame at the age of fifteen and was in that same department until he retired. John was Burnley born and bred and attended North Street School before leaving at the age of twelve to take up full time employment at the mill. He had plenty of plans for his retirement days ahead – John was a keen Burnley Football Club fan; he even saw the team win the cup at Crystal Palace in 1913–14. His other interests included horse racing, and he was a member of the Homing Society Working Men's Club just off Briercliffe Road for twenty-three years.

DEAN MILL, PLUMBE STREET, BURNLEY

Dean Mill was built around 1903, and worked by Luke Thornber Ltd in 1945, which was operating 720 looms. Dean Mill is located above the former tannery on Plumbe Street. The mill still survives and has been extensively renovated in recent years, now used by small industrial units. At one time it was used as a saw mill. Luke Thornber was Sharp Thornber's youngest brother (he who operated Park Shed on Leyland Road): both members of the Thornber family went on to become great cotton manufacturers in Burnley. Luke went into cotton manufacture first at Healey Wood Mill, and then he began on his own account at Dean Mill. Perhaps Luke's little-known claim to fame was the 'Great Walking Match', an event which took place on 11 May 1907 between Luke and Herbert Grey, the husband of Caleb Thornber's daughter. The race was over a distance of about sixteen and a half miles between Nelson and Whalley via the Nick of Pendle. A small book privately published in Burnley Reference Library describes the 'Great Walking Match' in a hilarious way, with accounts of the training undertaken by the competitors, the stake, which consisted of four teas, the route to be taken and the race itself. This was won by Herbert Grey by a lead of 300 yards in spite of having given Luke a quarter of an hour lead. Another member of the Thornber Dynasty, who practically owned all of the looms in the Burnley area, was the well-known and highly respected Titus Thornber, the Cliviger local historian who died in 2006. His knowledge of the local landscape around Cliviger led him to write the definitive book on the area, *A Pennine Parish – The History of Cliviger*: he will be sadly missed.

Dean Mill.

ELM STREET MILL, ELM STREET, BURNLEY

The following description was given to Elm Street Mill when trading as W. Melland, but when owned by B.M. Melland:

These commodious premises are situated on a main highway (Elm Street) which is in an industrious zone about one mile from Burnley centre in East Lancashire. The whole of this large building is of good quality red-brick terraced at varying heights along its frontage with ornamental sandstone slabs and a 'Sailor' coursed parapet. This frontage with an overall length of 478 feet, is of three storeyed construction with uniform floor areas at each level, but deranged at its centre by the boiler and engine rooms.

Furthermore, the frontage is angled at it centre to give one hundred and forty degrees, and this angular construction is maintained throughout the factory from back to front. The frontage is broken at ground level by three loading bays and runs north to south. The main factory is all single storeyed construction, carries a north light roofing system of bays which is carried by cast-iron pillars at approx., 21 foot centres. Internally, this factory area is subdivided in roughly equal halves by a main red bricked wall some 24 inches thick, and each of these halves is further divided by red brick walls four and a half inch thick. All these internal dividing walls are built with several pass-through doors of ample proportions. The factory chimney of octagonal design is 142 feet high, and is situated centrally with the powerhouse section. Generally speaking the whole of the building is of a fireproof design having non-combustible divisions throughout and is equipped with a fire escape at each end. It is serviced at regular intervals with four lifts each operating through all three floors. All main services of electricity, gas and towns water enter the building at many points, and toilet facilities are plentiful. The structure was begun in the early 1880s and is freehold for 999 years. The present rateable value is £5,881 per annum.

Elm Street Mill.

A steam engine here was made by Galloways Ltd of Manchester in 1926 and worked until the mill closed down in 1967. The engine was donated to the Museum of Science and Industry in 1970 by Mr B. Melland, a relative of the original owners of Elm Street Mill. The flywheel on this huge engine could accommodate eighteen driving ropes. The Elm Street Mill still survives to this day, being used by various small firms. The chimney mentioned above appears to have been reduced in height. William Bird was one of the occupiers of the Elm Street Mill just after the Second World War, when he was operating 128 looms.

ELM STREET SHED, ELM STREET

Elm Street was worked by James Lee and Brothers in 1923; Brown, Ridehalgh and Glover in 1940 with forty-eight looms, and the Elm Street manufacturing Co. Ltd in 1945. The latter firm operated 140 looms with cloth widths of 30in to 44in. A rather unique washhouse for use by the workpeople at the mills and sheds, owned by the Melland family, was opened at Elm Street Shed in 1926, by Councillor Melland. The washhouse contained two washers – one of which was capable of holding five family washes – along with twenty 'pull up' racks for drying the clothes.

EMPIRE MILL, LIVERPOOL ROAD

This mill was worked as a weaving mill by Arthur Edmondson Ltd in 1945 and in 1962, according to trade directories. Arthur Edmondson also ran the Fir Trees Mill at Higham. The two mills worked 1,400 looms, manufacturing coloured stripes, rayon, two and three fold yarns and fancy dobby clothes. This mill was built in 1910 and survived until quite recently, being the mill nearest Liverpool Road, beyond the canal towards Lowerhouse. It was a predominately red-bricked weaving mill with fancy stone coping stones, used just prior to demolition, by a number of small industrial units.

The mill was demolished within the past five years. In 2007 it was announced that the site would be brought back into use as a new industrial estate and housing, creating hundreds of jobs.

EXTWISTLE MILL, EXTWISTLE

This mill was romantically situated in the valley below Extwistle Hall. The mill, originally a corn mill, dated from around the 1370s, and later used for worsted manufacture. John Parker built the last mill in the seventeen century, and Peter Parker worked it in 1824. A few years later, around 1827, Heap and Holt were working the Extwistle Mill, and in 1844 James Greenwood took over the mill, and ran it until 1884. By the 1900s the mill was derelict. Only the foundations remain today and a number of large engine beds and the reed-filled mill lodge. Mr John Spencer recalled in *Reminiscences of Old Burnley*, (a series of articles in the *Burnley Express* from 13 May 1899), that on one occasion the great water wheel got jammed and stuck fast. The water was turned off, and Mr Spencer, then a boy of eight or nine, living at Lea Green was lowered by ropes into the mill race to set it free with a stick. See also *A Lancashire Township* by Roger Frost for a more detailed history of Extwistle Mill.

FERNDALE MILL, EASTERN AVENUE, BURNLEY

The Ferndale Mill, built in 1912 by Robert Emmott, was one of the last cotton mills to be built in Burnley. It held 1,476 looms, most of which came from Pemberton's, Waterloo Foundry on Trafalgar Street. It was worked by Robert Emmott in 1923 and 1945. Robert Emmott also worked the Stanley Mills not far away: altogether both mills operated 3,306 looms. The mill has now been demolished, and the remains can be seen at the back of the petrol station above Bancroft Road. The garage in fact backs on the wall that used to surround the mill, being built in red brick, with some nice ornamental work. To the left of the garage is a pair of fine ornamental wrought iron gate with roses, which are mounted on a pair of brick and stone gateposts. The gates still bear a notice, 'No unauthorised persons allowed on these premises. All enquiries at the office'. Just inside the gates steps, complete with handrails, give access to the remains of the mill. Only a small section of the walling now survives, along with the mill floor itself, at least in part. Forward, and on the left-hand side, is an admirable cast-iron beam with the words 'Ferndale Mill 1912' on what is left of the mill walls. Just inside the gates mentioned above was a single-storey office block with three windows, to the right of this was what appears to have been the engine-house over the door of which was the cast-iron beam mentioned above.

I'm afraid I don't known when Ferndale Mill was demolished, although it may have been taken over by Bellings. It appears to have survived until the 1960s at least. In April 1960, the borough surveyor received a request from Bellings 'for the provision of two toilets blocks at Ferndale Mill', and, 'B.Y. Jackson applied for permission to fill in the lodge at the mill'. Today the former mill site is used in the main as car parking for the nearby industrial estates.

FINSLEY MILL, FINSLEYGATE, BURNLEY

This is the mill with a somewhat chequered history, was later worked by Lambert Howarth and Sons, and is on the right-hand side of Finsleygate before the Canal Bridge. It was worked by Witham Brothers in 1945, who along with their Plumbe Street Shed worked 43,000 spindles and 1,540 looms.

There was a horrific boiler explosion at what was termed Finsley Mill, which was reported in the *Burnley Advertiser* on 1 September 1852. A huge volley of steam, fire, boiling hot water, and hot ashes engulfed several people. No less than eleven persons were found to have been injured, four of them so seriously that they died during the night or during the following morning. Those killed for the sake of genealogists were: William Winterbottom, aged twenty-nine years; George Whitaker, aged seventeen; Joseph Townson aged fifty-seven and John Thornton aged thirty-one. The injured were George Whitaker, Coke Street; William Watson, Coke Street; Samuel Bracewell, Lanebridge; Robert Heys, Lanebridge; Richard Jackson, Lanebridge, and Peter Robinson, of Sandy Gate. The mill was let in 1857, although the mill itself might have been the earlier structure, known as 'Turn Bridge Mill' shown on the 1851 map, and built by the Holgate's around 1820. John and George Holgate were listed as being 'cotton spinners and manufacturers at Turn-bridge Mill, in 1843. The 'Turn Bridge', or swing-bridge, operated here until the building of the canal bridge in 1886.

Certainly the Finsley Mill was in existence in 1848 and 1866, when it worked by Henry Knowles and Sons, cotton spinners and manufacturers. A date stone on the Finsleygate side in fact reads 'FINSLEY 1866', although it is somewhat difficult to spot – laying just above the roof of the single floor section near road. At this time, it was worked by Henry Knowles and contained about 30,000 spindles, and the machinery was 'nearly new and of the best description' which implies a recent structure. It was at Finsley Mill that George Keighley served his apprenticeship as an engineer. George later went on to become a major loom manufacturer in the town, an alderman, and mayor, and a founder of the Victoria Hospital. The Finsley Mill has nothing special to compliment it – it was built simply as a cotton-spinning mill, stout and sturdy, but nothing fancy. James Baron and Sons, Cotton and Cotton-Waste Merchants, were working at Finsley Mill in the 1920s. This firm was founded in 1831, and made into a limited company in 1907, supplying cotton-waste of all grades for spinning, cleaning waste and surgical wadding. The firm was also the proprietors of the Barchant Spinning Co. of Rochdale and Besco Co. at Rochdale, manufacturers of the Besco brushes and mops. Josuah Hoyle and Sons finished at Finsley Mill in 1958, and cotton manufacture was brought to an end. It was two years later, in 1960, that Lambert Howarth and Sons took over the premises. Cuckoo Mill on Blackburn Street is considered by many to be the oldest mill in Burnley in its original form: however, some parts of the Finsley Mill date back to the 1820s. It was estimated that some £20,000 worth of damage was caused to the mill in March 1866, when fire almost gutted the factory. A novel way of trying to extinguish the flames was brought into use – the breaking of the steam pipes in the factory. The steam engulfed the fire, and to some extent quelled the flames. One fatality was reported, however, that of an eleven-year-old creeler at the mill named Benjamin Pounder. The lad was seen to leave the mill after the fire had started, but returned for his jacket, and was not seen again.

FOUNDRY STREET MILL

This mill is on Foundry Street, the old name for that end of Finsleygate nearest to Manchester Road, and operated from around 1810 to around 1830. The mill stood about where the car salesroom is today; there are of course no remains.

FULLEDGE MILL, TODMORDEN ROAD, BURNLEY

The Fulledge Mill was on the opposite side of the River Calder Bridge to Hand Bridge Mill. William Halstead, who hailed from Harle Syke, built the mill in 1854, it being completed 1856.

Finsley Mill.

The date stone of Finsley Mill.

It was worked by John Garstang in 1887 with fifty-two looms and by J.W. Smith in 1923. The mill was partially destroyed in a fire in October 1915. Shortly after the mid-1920s there followed a great depression in the cotton trade, and Fulledge mill, then worked by H. Bracewell, had over forty looms stopped, and Whitehead and Leaver had 345 looms stopped.

By 1934, the Fulledge Mill was occupied by Windle and Co. and Charles Taylor, but by 1937 there was a newspaper report that Fulledge Mill was to close, (see below). The mill appears to have been demolished in 1971, when the date stone was salvaged, but for some reason buried behind Towneley Hall. The site of Fulledge Mill is now a car valet place and other small business establishments and only a few of the walls survive. An extract from the *Burnley Express* 23 October 1937:

Fulledge Mill to close. About 100 operatives thrown out of work. Fulledge Mill Holmes Street which was owned by Mr Joseph Thomas Sutcliffe who died last March will close down next weekend. The mill contains 734 looms but 260 of these have been stopped since about February, and from that time a gradual working out process has been in operation. About 100 work people will be thrown out of employment as a result of the stoppage next week...

GANNOW SHED, OFF GANNOW LANE, TO THE REAR OF YATEFIELD MILL

The shed dated from 1867, and in 1887 it was worked by the Burrows Brothers, when they had 613 looms in operation. 680 looms here were 'stopped' during a great depression in the cotton trade between 1922 and 1834. It was later occupied by the Walton Brothers, and then by T. Redman and Co., provisions merchants. There are no remains of Gannow Shed – the site was cleared during the construction of the M65 motorway.

GEORGE STREET SHED, GEORGE STREET, BURNLEY

This was originally part of the Burnley Iron Works, and consisted of an open yard with a smithy, part of the Burnley Iron Works itself. William Bracewell took over the iron works around 1876, and built over the open yard to form the George Street Shed. In doing so he covered over a canalside dock connected with the iron works. A tramway ran from the open yard through a couple of tunnels to the dock, presumably to carry away the produce by canal. These two tunnel can still be seen at the back of what is now the Newtown Works on the Sandygate side. By 1879, Henry Bracewell, (his son?) a cotton manufacturer was at George Street Shed. William Bracewell was also listed in this year as operating the Queen Street Mill (Burnley). William Bracewell came from the wealthy family of Bracewell Hall, Bracewell Village, near Barnoldswick, and he went on to become one of Burnley's great industrialists, particularly in connection with the Burnley Iron Works. Part of this still survives and it became the Newtown Steel Works in 1949. George Street Shed was to be let on a 'room and power' basis for 500 looms in 1897. The George Street Shed was worked by John Stansfield and Son Ltd in 1923 and in 1945 – running 966 looms – and also Dennis Berry Ltd operated here in the latter year. The mill still survives, although in April 2007 it suffered badly in a fire believed to have been started by arsonists, which destroyed the third floor of the old mill. Another claim to dubious fame at the George Street Shed is that this was the mill where one of Burnley's war heroes, Pte Richard Smith, worked before being killed in October 1918, just three weeks before the end of the war. His medals, the British War and Victory Medals, were put up for auction in London in April 2005.

GOODHAM HILL MILL, GOODHAM HILL, BURNLEY

This is the name given to the portion of St James' Street between Hammerton Street and Cow Lane, also known as 'Tunstill's Mill'. The mill was being worked by Thomas Howarth in 1843 and by Henry Tunstill in 1848, and the Tunstill Brothers were working the Goodham Hill Mill in 1868, as cotton spinners and manufacturers. Thomas Tunstill is recorded as living at No. 25 Ashfield Road in the early 1880s, and his occupation was listed as a cotton manufacturer. Obviously nothing remains of this old mill: the area has long since been developed. The mill was in the area later occupied by the later Empire Cinema, and shops such as the Empire News and those to the corner of Cow Lane, and to the rear of these buildings as far as the alleyway. It was stated that 'vegetables on sale at the Victoria Market (Hammerton Street/St James' Street) were constantly covered with dirt and grit from the 'blow hole' and chimney of Tunstill's Mill'.

John Spencer also operated a mill at Goodham Hill in 1824, and a steam engine was installed at a mill at Goodham Hill before 1800. Mr Spencer was described as being a very distinguished gentleman of fine appearance. He always wore a suit of broadcloth, an unusual thing for a layman in those days. He also sported a heavy watch, chain and seal. The council purchased Tunstill's Mill in 1882 for £8,000, and demolished the building to remove the 'bottleneck' in the road. We have a few more details of the Goodham Mill from the *London Gazette* of 24 April 1819, which said:

> To be sold by auction in pursuant to an order of the Chancery Court of Lancashire in a case of Richard William Moxon and others. John Hartley and others at the Black Bull Inn, Burnley in the County of Lancashire on May 21st.
>
> Lot 1. All that commodious freehold cotton mill situated at Goodham Hill in Burnley, about 40 yards long by 23 yards wide together with a steam engine of 22 hp, shafts, drums, wheels etc. The mill adjoins to and is abundantly supplied with water from the River Calder, and is situated within the township of Burnley.

The obituary of Thomas Hardacre in July 1916 tells the tale of an extremely remarkable man. Thomas recalled working in a mill when he was six years of age from six in the morning until eight thirty at night – on one occasion putting in a ninety-two hour week for the grand sum of two shillings. At sixteen years of age, Thomas went to work in a mill at Ingleton in Yorkshire, and each Saturday would walk home back to Burnley – a distance of over twenty-eight miles – and return on the Sunday night, rain or shine. Thomas came to Burnley around 1847 and found work at Tunstill's Mill. About 1854 he helped 'gait up' the Fulledge Mill for Mr Halstead, and remained there for twenty-four years. He could also remember the introduction of the steam looms, and when the hand-loom weavers drew the plugs from the boilers, and the soldiers had to be called out – a remarkable man indeed.

In February 1855, there was a fatal accident at what was called 'the new end of Messrs Tunstill's Mill at Goodham Hill'. Two bays of the fire-proof flooring at the mill, which was four storeys high, gave way, taking with it two bricklayers named Samuel Massey and Henry Haworth. The latter survived, but Massey was unfortunately found dead among the debris.

GRIMSHAW STREET MILL

A mill on Grimshaw Street, Burnley, worked from around 1840 through to 1874. Nothing remains – the area has long since been redeveloped.

Habergham Mill.

HABERGHAM MILL, COAL CLOUGH LANE, BURNLEY

Habergham Mill was worked by T.R. and H. Emmott and Curedale in 1923, but only A. Curedale Ltd by the mid-1940s. This latter firm operated 544 looms of 24in to 34in wide manufacturing twills, satteens and jeanettes. Mr Plumbridge, whose wife was a Curedale before her marriage, had a son who began hand-printing cotton material with a friend on a small scale here. The rest of the place was taken up by Lucas for storage. There was a disastrous fire at the Habergham Mill in March 1931, when it was run by Curedale's, but the mill recovered. T. Foster Ltd, cotton manufacturer was also listed as working the Habergham Mill in 1923 and in 1962. During 1944–46, the Habergham Mill was acquired by Lucas to assist the Wood Top Works in the production of gas turbine equipment, but later reverted back to cotton weaving.

The mill was weaving cotton until around the late 1960s, as a 'room and power company', shared between the firms of Foster's and Curedale's. The Clarkson's (of Clarkson and Sutcliffe) managed and partly owned the Foster's firm. Habergham Mill was originally begun in 1913 (see date stone), when the mill engine was christened, and the works opened in February that year. The mill is on the left-hand side of Coal Clough Lane up the second turn-off after Cog Lane before Rossendale Road. The mill survives to this day.

HALL RAKE MILL, HALL STREET, BURNLEY

Hall Rake is the old name for Hall Street; 'rake' simply means steep incline. The mill here was at the bottom of Hall Street on the right-hand side, and it was worked by Kershaw and Waring and Co. in 1865. The mill, a cotton-spinning mill dating from around 1840, was owned by Henry Dixon. It was built, so we are told by Walter Bennett in his *History of Burnley* (Vol. III page 176), on grammar school land. Nothing remains today, although some arches belonging to the former mill were visible until the 1960s. The Hall Rake Mill 'machinery and utensils' were offered for sale by auction in the *Burnley Advertiser* on 23 June 1877. It was advertised again in the local newspaper on 6 December 1884:

> Sale of Mill Property. Mr Matthew Watson on Monday evening offered at the Bull Hotel, Hall Rake Mill and adjoining shops in Church Street. No sale was effected in public, but immediately afterwards the mill was sold to Mr John Greenhalgh, fruit preserver for £2,505 or £5 over the reserve bid, and the other property to the same gentleman for £2,100. Messrs Backhouse and Proctor were the solicitors in the matter.

HANDBRIDGE MILL, PARLIAMENT STREET, BURNLEY

Handbridge Mill dates from around 1844, and was built by Norton Fletcher, a plumber and glazier, and is marked on the 1851 map. It takes its name from a building near to the bottom entrance to Towneley Hall, or as tradition states, from some handloom weavers' cottages close by. Hartley Jackson worked the mill in 1923, although a part was used by Joseph R. Smith as a cotton-waste merchant. By 1934, the mill was in the hands of the Parliament Manufacturing Co. and its 440 looms were 'stopped'. The Coal Street Waste Co. Ltd (a firm founded in 1933) was working the Handbridge Mill in 1945. All types of cotton-waste were handled by this firm for re-spinning and making engine cloths. The mill, after being extensively renovated, is now used by the firm 'Premier Gas'.

HARGHER CLOUGH MILL, HARGHER STREET, BURNLEY

Built as a cotton-weaving shed around 1882, when it was reported in March that year that 'Walmsley's Shed at Wood Top was ready for roofing'. The mill was built by John Walmsley and his son George, who later went on to built his own mill, named Peel Mill on Gannow Lane. The Hargher Clough Mill is still with us, and is the mill on Hargher Street just above Howard Street at Wood Top. It dates from 1881–82. A large 'mill pond' used to exist near the top of Bruce Street in connection with the Hargher Clough Mill. The factory was worked by Thomas Cowpe and Sons Ltd in 1923. At the end of 1940, the Hargher Clough Mill was taken over by Lucas, and used for the production of aircraft generators, starter motors and rotary converters. The Lucas business was founded by Joseph Lucas in 1887, and one of the first products of the firm was that of ship's lamps. From this modest workshop, and due to the excellent products produced, the Lucas Organisation went on to employ over 55,000 people nation-wide.

The year following 1940 saw the organisation take over the running of Northbridge Works, and the Wood Top Mill. On a cold January morning in 1919, young twelve-year-old James Berry and his friend took his father's dinner to the mill. Having given the dinner to his father, the two began playing around in a store room attached to Hargher Clough Mill. The mill hoist proved beyond temptation for the two adventurers, and while messing around on the lift young James became trapped between the shaft wall and the lift, and was killed.

Dinner time in Parliament Street. (courtesy of the Briercliffe Society)

Hargher Clough Mill.

HARLE SYKE MILL, HARLE SYKE

Worked by the Oxford Mill Co. Ltd in 1962. A steam engine here built in and installed by the Burnley Iron Works in 1904 was removed to the Science Museum in London, where it can still be seen working. The mill was built in parts, the first section being commenced in 1855/56. Harle Syke Mill consists of two weaving sheds, the 'Top Shop' and the 'Bottom Shop' which is the older part of the weaving sheds. The older section of the mill was built by local handloom weavers fearing that the power looms would force them out of work. The mill survives, being used today by small industry.

HEALEY ROYD MILL, HEALEY WOOD ROAD, BURNLEY

John and James Sellers, cotton spinners and manufacturers were working this mill in 1848, and in 1868. It was worked by the Burnley Self Help Ltd from around 1887 through to around 1923, in shared premises, which were also let out and worked by a number of other firms. These included the Healey Royd Manufacturing Co. Ltd, F. Horne and Co. and Kippax and Redman. During a depression in the cotton trade in the 1920s and '30s the Burnley Self Help Ltd had sixty-four looms which were 'stopped'. This huge weaving shed contains a floor space of 13,250 yards, and has a site area of 10,000 yards. In the mid-1930s, the power to the mills was provided by two Lancashire boilers that provided the steam for a 650hp double-beam engine with gear drive. The firm of Lambert and Howarth moved into these premises in March 1939. It's worth noting here that in 1800 a Joseph Watson had a weaving factory at Burnley Wood, which might have been Healey Royd, and bought jenny-spun yarn at 4d a pound. In early 2007 a plan for a £10 million redevelopment of Victorian Healey Royd canalside mills were submitted to the council. Under the proposals Healey Royd Mill would be converted into fifty-two one- and two-bedroom apartments.

HEALEY WOOD MILL

Healey Wood Road was where the industrial units are today off Healey Wood Road; nothing remains of the actual mill. The Healey Wood Mill dated from around 1845, although it was rebuilt in 1881. The Healey Wood Mill Co. Ltd worked the mill in the 1920s, and the 1940s. It shows up on a map for the year 1851, and may have originally been a worsted mill, which was advertised in the *Burnley Advertiser* on 2 October 1875 as:

> Healey Wood Worsted Mills Burnley. To be sold by private treaty, the whole of the above premises consisting of a 4 storey mill, 4 two storey warehouses, 2 one storey warehouses, loom shed capable of containing 250 looms, engine house, boiler house and reservoir, together with the engine, boiler shafting, gearing gas and steam pipes throughout.

The mill finished in or around 1967 and was demolished in 1971. On 25 May 1971, the *Burnley Express* reported an explosion at Healey Wood, which occurred while demolition work was in progress at the mill. Workers on the contract were using explosives to destroy a tank at the mill, used as part of its fire-fighting apparatus. Residents had

Healey Royd Mill.

Healey Mill.

been warned of the blast, but it was bigger than expected. A flying brick hit a senior police officer on the knee, and bricks were sent flying, shattering the windows of the Healey Wood Inn.

A long-serving weaver here at the mill was James Hirst of No. 70 Parliament Street who retired in 1937 after completing fifty years service. They gave out some rather strange retirement gifts in those days – James was presented with a fireside chair and a clock by his workmates, and a cheque from the management.

HEASANDFORD MILL, HEASANDFORD, BURNLEY

The Heasandford Mill dates from 1904, and had the honour of being the first shed in England to be run by electricity. The mill was worked by the Heasandford Manufacturing Co. Ltd 1945 (and 1962), who were running 1,679 looms. Much of the mill still survives, although it is true to say that much has also been demolished. The buildings are brick built with some fancy stonework and arches. The firm of 'Tarmac', and a number of small firms, occupy the rear of the mill today, while at the front is Altham's Travel – a branch of the original firm. Learoyd Packaging occupies a section further up the river with new extensions. The original Heasandford Mill was a water-powered corn mill later converted to cotton manufacturing and was much nearer the main road, around the site of the mining memorial in Bank Hall Park, and ran from around 1820 to the 1870s. There are no remains of this mill, although the mill race can be traced in part running up through the woods to the left and rear of the present Heasandford Mill. In January 1971, a fierce blaze caused £120,000 worth of damage at the present Heasandford Mill.

HIGHER RAKE HEAD MILL

This was probably part of Rake Head Mill, and dates from around 1840. Nothing remains.

HILL END MILL

This mill was at Lower Bank Parade: worked from 1841, it was rebuilt in 1870 and survived until 1955 as a cotton-waste establishment. The Hill End Mill was worked by the Fishwick family, and stood where the post office sorting office is today. Webster Fishwick worked a mill named 'Bank' as a cotton spinner and manufacturer in 1818–1820. The name might imply that it also was in this district, or even another name for the Hill End Mill? By the 1920s this establishment was in the occupation of William Lancaster, a cotton-waste merchant.

HILL END MILL, LANE BOTTOM, BRIERCLIFFE

This was an old woollen mill built in around 1777, and operated by William Smith in the handloom era; it has now been demolished. Power looms were introduced at the Hill End Mill in 1838, when it progressed to employing over 200 people. In the 1851 census William was described as a 'Power Loom Manufacturer' and employed eighty-nine men, forty-five women, thirty-five boys and thirty-two girls. The mill was put up for sale in May 1905, and it included 428 power looms, three cop-winding machines, four beaming engines, a tape-sizing machine, a

Tom and Harold Nuttall at Hill End Mill, Haggate, 1905. (courtesy of the Briercliffe Society)

Hill End Mill. (courtesy of the Briercliffe Society)

cloth-plaiting machine, and a cloth press. There were also two steam engines, the main one of which drove the machinery, and a smaller 'donkey engine', probably for the sizing machine. The mill was sold to William Nuttall for £4,700 acting on behalf of the workpeople. The play area at Lane Bottom now occupies most of the site of the former mill. Much of this information and that of other Briercliffe mills are from Roger Frost's *A Lancashire Parish*. The mill does show up in a cotton trades' directory for the year 1940, when it was being worked by the 'Hill End Mill Co. Ltd (1905)' which was running 480 looms manufacturing bleachers, printers and jeans.

HILL TOP MILL, HILL TOP, BURNLEY

Now demolished, this was to the rear of the Rishton Mill, and on Hill Top Street; the area was all demolished in the mid-1930s. Today the area would have been around where the first Sainsbury's store was located before being moved to nearer Bank Top. The mill was built around 1820, and run by John and George Barnes. The mill shows up on a map for the year 1851. By 1841 the mill was being run by Gorge Barnes and Brothers. Messrs J. and C. Sutcliffe were working the mill in 1868, and the Hill Top Mill Co. was formed in 1875. The secretary of the Hill Top Mill Co. at this time was Tom Holroyd, a cotton spinner who lived at No. 74 Todmorden Road. The Hill Top Mill Co. was also working the Hill Top Mill in the 1930s; however, they had over 650 looms stopped due to a depression in trade, and the mill was demolished shortly afterwards. It was while the Hill Top Mill Co. were running the mill that there was a fatal accident there. In May 1907, twenty-five-year-old Arthur Nicholls of Adland Street went to tighten a nut on top of the mill boiler when it burst off. Arthur was immediately covered in scalding steam and hot water: he was quickly attended to, but later died in hospital – just one of many mill fatalities.

HOLLINGREAVE MILL

This mill was on Job Street, off Finsleygate. It is possibly another name for the Lane Bridge Mill, a nut and bolt works in later years (?). An Edward Gregson was working a mill in Lane Bridge in 1818–1820 as a cotton manufacturer and spinner.

HOPE MILL, TRAFALGAR STREET

Hope Mill was operated in the late 1870s by Thomas Carr, cotton manufacturer, and built for him in 1874. This is the mill that still survives and which presents the look of a blank wall at the bottom end of Burnham Gate, as you wait for the traffic lights to change. Thomas Carr was born in Rossendale around 1829 and by 1881 was employing 110 hands at his mills. Thomas and his wife Ann lived at No. 185 Manchester Road, Burnley at this time.

HOWE STREET MILL, HOWE STREET

This mill and its location is recalled in Howe Walk, and was at the St James's Street end of the old Market Hall. The mill here operated from around 1820, but only for about ten years. Mills in the Market Place and Keighley Green were being worked by Thomas Kay in 1818–1820 – might this have been Howe Street Mill?

Imperial Mill, Rosegrove

This survived until only a few years ago, and was worked by John Spencer (Burnley) Ltd in 1923 and 1945. The mill was in fact built by John Spencer in 1905, commencing operations in 1906, and was on the left-hand side of Rosegrove (Dugdale) Canal Bridge going down towards Lane Ends. The mill contained 1,278 looms in the 1930s. Imperial Mill was predominately a red-bricked weaving shed with sandstone inserts with various extensions and used by small industrial units until it was demolished. From around 2004 the area around the mill was a constant source of trouble – local youths vandalised the small businesses which occupied Imperial Mill. The date stone, which was on the canal elevation, had the date '1905' and the name 'Imperial Mill' written in stone. The much discussed and despised 'six loom per weaver' system was started at the Imperial Mill in September 1931. The system was originally based on an eight looms per weaver system, but after many demonstrations, the former was finally accepted.

Industry Mill, Stanley Street, Burnley

Worked by John S. Veevers, cotton spinners and manufacturers, in 1887 and 1890. The Industry Mill closed in the later year, and was built around 1840. John Sharples Veevers was born at Burnley in 1833, and lived at Reedley, he was a J.P. and former Burnley Guardian, and he died in 1905. The Industry Mill, colloquially known as Smithfield Mill, was located on land that is now used as car parking at the corner of Stanley Street and Cooper Street, under the Centenary Way 'flyover', and takes it name from a former mill owner here named Thomas Henry Smith. By the 1920s, Industry Mill was a cotton-waste shop in the occupation of William Lancaster, who also had premises at Cooper Street across the way and on Bank Parade, at the factory formerly run by the Fishwick family.

Jewel Mill, Reedley

Jewel Mill was between Greenhead Lane and Quaker Bridge, besides Pendle Water and down Barden Lane. The original Jewel Mill was built as a water-powered mill in 1828, but this was demolished sometime after 1886. Robert Shaw is listed as working Jewel Mill in 1865. Another mill was built on the same site in around 1890, and in later years it was owned by Lockwood, Buckley Ltd and used as a weaving and spinning mill. At the start of the Second World War the firm was running 8,000 spindles. However, this 'new' mill also succumbed to 'progress' – being demolished around 1979 to make way for the new motorway, the M65. Plans were afoot to make this into an industrial museum for the area, but they came to no fruition. All that remains now is the mill dam and water race upstream, near Quaker Bridge. In April 1886 it was stated that 'Jewel Mill which is in the occupancy of Messrs Shaw of Colne will be shortly vacated by the tenants. The removal of the machinery has already commenced'.

Keighley Green Mill

The Keighley Green Mill was built prior to 1851, showing up on a map for that year, and finished cotton spinning in 1914. Following this all the machinery was sold off, notably to

James Dixon, a scrap merchant who at this time had his yard next to the canal bridge on Briercliffe Road, just past the entrance to Bank Hall, but on the other side of the road. In February 1916, James Dixon and a number of his men were removing some old boilers, each weighing around ten tons at the Keighley Green Mill. They had just got the second boiler out of the boiler room into the mill yard, which was some yards higher than the boiler house itself. They began inching the boiler towards a waiting wagon along the level mill yard. Suddenly, the boiler slipped to one side, trapping one man. The man, Ernest Green, was instantly killed by the boiler: two others were injured. Alfred Whitfield had his shoulder broken, and the man in charge, James Dixon, had his shoulder crushed. The Keighley Green Mill was later worked by Leather Garments (Burnley) Ltd, a firm incorporated in 1947. They moved to Keighley Green in 1957, producing industrial ladies', men's and youth's jeans. This mill has now been demolished, but was just above the old Bridge Street Mill. The back of the Keighley Green Mill in fact faced the old Market Tavern.

KING'S MILL, BRIDGE STREET, BURNLEY

This mill replaced the old King's Mill, a corn mill dating from around 1290. This burnt down in 1852, and in its place was built the new King's Mill by Spencer and Moore. This partnership consisted of John Moore, who later became the town's first mayor, and his wife's brother, John Spencer, and was founded around the early 1820s. This John Spencer is no relation to John Spencer (Burnley) Ltd mentioned elsewhere. At the time of the rebuilding of King's Mill, the partnership was at its highest peak.

In 1854, their great new mill, Parsonage Mill, on Keighley Green, was nearing completion. John Moore was a well-respected businessman, and during the Cotton Famine did all he could to help his workers, making a donation of £25 each month to the Relief Funds. Various trade and labour problems beset the partnership, even after the worst of the Cotton Famine. In September 1866, most of John Moore's property was up for sale: these included Palace House, the family home, Lower Hood House and Parsonage Mill. Samuel Howard bought most of the property, and leased the Parsonage Mill back to John Moore, but its days were numbered. John Moore died at Nelson House off Manchester Road in October 1869. In 1876, a headstone was erected at his grave, provided by his successive mayors as a mark of their esteem. Nothing remains of King's Mill, or for that matter Parsonage Mill: all were swept aside by redevelopment. Henry Milne and Co. are listed as working the King's Mill in 1865. In its latter years the King's Mill was occupied by Nuttall and Co., a printing firm.

KING'S MILL, HARLE SYKE

Worked by Mason, West and Bather Ltd in 1962, this firm was running 1,013 looms in 1940. The King's Mill was the last mill to be built in Briercliffe in 1912/13 by George Mason. The mill has a fine stone frontage with some fancy stonework, and a red-brick chimney. The red-brick weaving shed is to the rear with a water tank, and is now used by the firm of King's Mill Antiques. This firm was started in 1997 by Michael and Linda Heuer, and has a thriving export business, as well as the home market. Part of the King's Mill was also used as a call centre, which closed with a loss of 160 jobs in 2005.

King's Mill, Burnley. (courtesy of the Briercliffe Society)

King's Mill, Harle Syke.

LANE BRIDGE MILL, JOB STREET, FINSLEYGATE, BURNLEY

This weaving shed was located on Job Street, now gone. The mill was off Finsleygate on the left-hand side going towards the canal. R.P. Woodward and Co., cotton manufacturers, worked the mill in the 1920s. The latter firm was still at the mill in 1934: however, its 532 looms were 'stopped'. Mrs E. Woodward of Adelaide Road, Hampstead owned the mill, which had a floor space of 3,000 yards in 1935, when the mill was up for sale at a selling price of £750, open to offers. The mill was said to be stone-built with slate roof, but in a dilapidated condition. Lane Bridge is the old name for this part of Finsleygate, and the mill dated from at least around the 1820s. However, in 1858, 'a very slight falling off in demand brought about financial difficulties for the owners of Lane Bridge Mill'. The mill had been demolished by 1945, when only Hartley and Baldwin Ltd, bolt manufacturers, are listed as being on Job Street.

LIVINGSTONE MILL, CAMERON STREET, BURNLEY

The Livingstone Mill was started along with its engine in April 1888: the building work commenced in 1886, and the wall bears the date stone '1887'. This and the Cameron Mill were both being worked by John Grey Ltd, in 1923, and 1945. It closed down as John Grey's in 1960, and was later taken over by the council, but at the time of writing it is used by small industrial units. Look for the paved cart road besides Livingstone Mill that runs down towards the canal. The mill is two storeys, built of red brick and still survives.

Livingstone Mill.

The date stone of Livingstone Mill.

Lodge Mill in 2007.

The fire at Lodge Mill.

Lodge Mill, advertising its famous product.

LODGE MILL, BARDEN LANE, BURNLEY

The Lodge Mill dated from 1863, and in 1865 was worked by James Stephen Birley. The mill was named originally Barden Mill, and took its 'Lodge Mill' name from the nearby Barden Lodge farm just over the canal. The Lodge Farm is on the left-hand side going down towards the bridge over Pendle Waters. It was the largest and oldest farm in Barden, and in the fifteenth century had a few acres in Oliver Ings (a name still used), Sand Banks (Pendle Bridge), Holme (Holme End), and an unknown Sagar Place.

The present house incorporates a well-proportioned farmstead, which was rebuilt in 1874 to replace a much older one. The Exors of Thomas Birley were working the mill in 1887 with 37,000 spindles. The mill was almost entirely gutted in a fire on Sunday 22 October 1905 – a fire that provided a spectacle watched by hundreds on the canalside. It took two days for the mill to burn down, and over 200 operatives lost their jobs. The mill was brought back into use, although the floors had to be lowered, and was worked by the Haythornthwaite Brothers in 1945, who were running 920 looms, and who also worked the Mount Pleasant Mill. Walter Haythornthwaite was the son of Thomas, a dairyman, and Mary, and was born at Wavertree Liverpool 12 December 1877 – he went on to become the managing director of the firm T. Haythornthwaite. From Anderton Terrace in Liverpool the whole family moved to Burnley to find work as weavers. Eventually in 1908 they were able to commence business on their own account in a small way at Meadow Bank Mill at Brierfield. The business prospered and in 1919 the firm moved to Lodge Mill, Barden Lane. It was Walter Haythornthwaite who invented, in 1923, what was to become the famed 'Grenfell cloth' which was specially made for Sir Wilfred Grenfell of Labrador and which was used on the Mount Everest expedition. In 1933, a Grenfell tent formed the highest habitation ever made by man on this planet. F.S. Smythe slept in it for thirteen hours and awoke 'fit and refreshed'. Up to this time scientists had predicted that any man sleeping at that altitude would never awaken. The tent was pitched at 27,000ft, in a blizzard that drove Smythe to his knees – a wind so strong that it forced microscopic snow crystals through other tents pitched 500ft below – but not through the Grenfell cloth. By the 1940s Walter Hayhornthwaite had moved to No. 10 Cavendish Road at St Annes-on-Sea, although for many years before this he lived at No. 22 Albert Street, Brierfield. It was at St Annes that Walter died, in May 1944. He was taken back for a service at Higham Methodist Chapel, a place to which he devoted much of his time. The Lodge Mill still survives across from the more famed Barden Mill.

LOWER RAKE HEAD MILL, RUSHWORTH STREET EAST, BURNLEY

Lower Rake Head Mill was worked by John Grey in the late 1870s. The mill survives, but is used for other light industries. The mill is a ramshackle collection of various buildings used as garages, a refrigeration engineer's, and part by Green Street Club. Burnley Caving Club used what was presumed to have been the old engine house for a number of years. Here, the high walls and solid stone sides made an excellent climbing wall and abseil tower for new cavers to practise on.

LOWERHOUSE MILLS, LOWERHOUSE

Lowerhouse Mills bore the inscription 'John, James and William Dugdale'. A more descriptive reading on these mills can be seen in Brian Hall's *Lowerhouse and the Dugdales*.

MARKET BRIDGE MILL, RIVER STREET, BURNLEY

The mill was up for sale by auction both in 1866 and 1870, and included steam engine, boilers, chimney, engine and boiler house, warehouse, iron water cistern shafting and gas and water pipes. The site covered 732 square yards and was calculated to hold 436 power looms or 10,000 mule spindles. It was occupied by the W. Mitchell, printer, stationer, and paper merchant, along with George Mitchell, electrical engineer (possibly related?) in 1923. The mill was demolished between this date and 1945, but the date stone still survives at the seating area above the Canal Bridge on Manchester Road. The name Market Street was the old name for that portion of Manchester Road from its junction with St James' Street to the Canal Bridge. It was renamed Manchester Road in May 1867.

MARKET STREET MILL

Little is known of this mill, other than it was in existence in around 1820. It may have been the Market Bridge Mill (see above).

MARLES SHED, LEE GREEN STREET, BURNLEY

This mill was around the present-day Lee Garden Street, Duke Bar, and was opened in 1865 and closed in 1934. In 1879 the mill was operated by James Heap, and in later years by Kippax and Sons, cotton manufacturers. James Heap was born in Colne around 1831, lived in Westgate and employed thirty-six persons at the Marles Shed. James married Ruth Smith at Burnley in 1854.

The shed had been demolished by the mid-1930s – nothing remains. The Marles Mill was originally a brick factory, and later the top room was used for spinning (according to Walter Bennett's *History of Burnley* Vol. III, page 182).

MARLFIELD MILL

This was worked by Mark Kippax and Sons in 1923, and was probably part of the Marles Shed. The mills took their name from Marles Farm that stood at the bottom end of Pheasantford Street, and Walshaw Street, whose fields were taken over by Bank Hall Colliery. Harry Birtwistle was the last tenant at Marles Farm about 1933. 'Marle' is a mixture of clay, limestone and silt and is used as a fertiliser.

MEADOW BANK MILL, HARLE SYKE

The Meadow Bank Mill had by 1934 been dismantled. It contained 850 looms and at this time was occupied by several firms.

MEADOWS MILL, GEORGE STREET, BURNLEY

Meadow Mill still survives: the premises is now occupied by Besglos Works. The mill is on the left-hand side, going over the footbridge to Trafalgar Street. The red-brick Meadows Mill dates from 1910, but was gutted by a huge fire in August 1949. At the time of the fire, the mill was being worked by G.E. Knowles (Bagmakers) Ltd and contained about 2,500 bags of raw cotton. It was rebuilt on the same site, a site that was previously occupied by the Walkerhey Mill.

MILL DAM MILL, BRIDGE STREET/HOWE STREET, BURNLEY

The Mill Dam Mill was operated by Crooke and Tattersall's, and dated from around 1780. It's worth noting here that the Sun Inn (later Hudson's leather shop) kept in 1880 by James Whittaker, not only had its own brewhouse, shippon and stables, but also a weaving shop fitted with handlooms. The Mill Dam Mill was worked by a waterwheel 3ft wide and 8ft high, turned by the water from the corn mill lodge behind the present-day Bridge Inn.

Behind the factory was a dwelling house, the town dungeon and two workshops above (according to Bennett's *History of Burnley*, part 3, page 175). There are no remains of the Mill Dam Mill: all this area has been redeveloped. Another name for the Mill Dam Mill might have been the Bridge Street Mill, this was advertised in October 1852 as:'To be let, Bridge Street Mill, room and power for 90–100 looms, also use of 60–90 looms if required'.

MOUNT PLEASANT, MILL MOUNT PLEASANT STREET, BURNLEY

Mount Pleasant Mill was located off Mount Pleasant Street, and between Whittam Street, (the area now occupied by the Crown Court). The mill was built prior to 1851, for it shows up on a map at this time, and in 1843 it was being worked by James Howorth, a worsted manufacturer, who lived on Hargreaves Street, but there are now no remains of the old mill.

The mill was begun as a worsted spinning mill named 'Howorth's', (or Howarth's) and extended over the decades. In 1877 the Mount Pleasant Mill failed through the troubles, with debts of £14,000. Shortly afterwards, the Mount Pleasant Mill was purchased by John Rawlinson, in 1878 in fact; it was refitted, and a new engine started. By 1885, part of the Mount Pleasant Mill was being worked by James Dilworth, Harrison and Brothers, and was 'four storeys high, thirteen windows long and five windows broad'. The bottom floor was used for skips and storage, the second floor for weaving, the third for additional storage and the forth for warping, winding and sizing. The mill employed around 350 hands.

Early on a Sunday morning on the 8 of March 1885, a weaver named George Shaw of Brown Street was passing the bottom end of Mount Pleasant Street when he saw smoke coming out of the building – he raised the alarm. The brigade was on the scene within minutes, but by now the flames were leaping from the building. It seemed at once that any effort to save the mill would be futile. The mill was soon gutted, within half an hour the roof caved in, the engine house was completely destroyed and the engine itself considerably damaged. The damage caused to the building was thought to have been around £10,000 to £12,000. The mill did restart, but it was estimated that it would take upwards of a month before the machinery could be repaired. The mill was worked by the Haythornthwaite Brothers in 1923 and in 1945, they also worked the Lodge Mill, Barden Lane. While the Haythornthwaite Brothers were at Mount Pleasant Mill they were operating 720 looms.

One of the managing directors of Haythornthwaite Brothers was Ephraim, who was born at Higham village. His first job was working part-time at the Fir Trees Mill just down the road from Higham village. He later got work at his father's and uncle's mills at Springhill Shed and Woodfield Mill at Burnley. It was in the year 1904 that he and his five older brothers decided to start up as manufacturers on their own account at Mount Pleasant Mill which became a limited company the following year. Naturally things were tight in the beginning, and they only had a few looms in operation, but slowly they were able to expand and in a short time they had 1,000 looms running. At the time of Ephraim's death 1953 the sheds at Mount Pleasant Mill had all been re-spaced but there were still 630 looms in operation. Mr Haythornthwaite like other Haythornthwaite's at Burnley, such as those who ran the Lodge Mill and produced the fame dGrenfell cloth, was brought back to his native Higham to be buried at the Wesley Chapel there. The old chapel itself has now been demolished, but many of the gravestones survive including those of the Haythornthwaites. The mill apparently closed down in December 1955, but must have reopened, for in 1962 it is listed as being worked by George Haythornthwaite Ltd. The mill has now been demolished.

The Mount Pleasant Mill was the place of a fatal accident in March 1914, when a young lad was killed playing football. John Southworth, aged thirteen years, along with a number of his workmates were playing a game with a ball made from cotton rags, as was usual during their dinner hour in a storeroom at the mill. For the goals they used the lift hoist shaft protected by some skips. John was in 'goal' and while diving to make a save, dislodged the skips and fell backwards down the hoist shaft, a distance of around 14ft. He later died as a result of the accident. While this incident might be considered to be extreme, it only goes to show that mill premises were just as dangerous as any other workplace.

Moorfield Mill, Standish Street, Burnley

This mill on Standish Street was said to be just sixteen yards by seven yards long, and two storeys high. Nothing remains: it was in operation from around 1844 to around 1858. The *Burnley Advertiser* for March 1853 included the following advert:

> For Sale. All that mill or power loom weaving shed called Moorfield Mill situated in and near back Standish Street, and lying between the line of that street and the River Brun, being two storeys high, 16 yards long and 7 yards wide or thereabouts with engine and boiler rooms over the latter now occupied as a shuttlemakers' shop and also a steam engine of 8hp...

New Hall Mill, Elm Street, Burnley

The New Hall Mill was the last mill on the left-hand side going down towards Livingstone Mill at the bottom end of Elm Street, just before the infant school. The New Hall Mill dates from 1877, and was erected by James and John Birley, who ran the mill until 1894, when it was taken over by the New Hall Mill Co. John and James were the sons of James Stephen Birley, a boat builder who gave his name to 'Birley's Dock, near the Colne Road canal bridge. James Stephen was born around 1881, later got involved in the cotton trade himself and lived at No. 64 Colne Road. He passed away at the ripe old age of seventy-three years and was buried in the family vault at St Peters' church, Burnley.

James Berry was also listed as a manufacturer at New Hall Mill in 1879 – he lived at No. 100 Manchester Road. While the Birley's were at New Hall Mill they had 53,006 spindles in operation. During a fire at the mill in October 1897, a policeman named Nuttall was killed under falling debris, and another injured; the damage caused by the fire amounted to £50,000. At the time of the fire the mill owners were in dispute with the workmen who called a strike and a number of 'knobstick' workers were brought in from out of town. When the fire was discovered these men, numbering around forty to fifty, were removed to a nearby joiner's shop. Occasionally some of them tried to 'escape' realising that their jobs were no longer secure, but the menacing attitude of the striking men outside forced them back. Later the men were taken to the Bank Top railway station under guard by a troop of policemen, to the hoots and cries from the crowd. Among the cries of 'knobsticks' and 'scabs', stones and other missiles were thrown, and there was a number of arrests before the strike breakers were placed safely on the train.

The ill-fated mill was the scene of another fatal accident around 1934: a workman was removing concrete from the bay of the fourth floor when it all collapsed around him, killing him instantly. In March the following year a twenty-seven-year-old Colne man met his death at the mill. The man, along with a companion, were employed in pulling down the mill chimney and were about to throw a stone from the top down to the ground. Suddenly, one of the men felt the chimney move beneath his feet: looking down he saw the coping stone giving way, and as it went it took with him the young man from Colne. The survivor was so shocked at the accident that it was some time before he was able to move and get himself down off the chimney to safety.

The mill was worked by W.C. Hargreaves, who had 370 looms 'stopped' during the depression of the 1930s, along with H. Tatham and Co., who had 240 looms stopped. By 1934, G. Wilkinson, Burnley Ltd, poultry appliance manufacturers, worked New Hall Mill. In 1956, the New Hall Mill was acquired by Lucas to assist in the production of motor-car electrical equipment. The mill survives to this day, although used for different purposes.

The New Hall Shed was sandwiched between the New Hall Mill and the North Bridge Mills and worked by Edwin Moore in 1868 as a cotton-spinning shed, and in 1879 by James Berry. The mill, also known as 'Birley's Mill' and was almost destroyed by fire in 1897, but was revived – being worked by William C. Hargreaves, in 1923. John Spencer (Burnley) Ltd and John Walton and Sons Ltd were working the New Hall Shed in 1945. The *Burnley Gazette* of 8 January 1870 bore the following article:

> Mr Matthew Watson begs to announce his instructions from Mr John Moore (who is declining business) to sell by auction at the weaving shed situated near New Hall, Burnley on Monday 10 January 1870, the following very excellent.
>
> Machinery and utensils namely, 244 power looms of 43 inch reed space by Bracewell and Bulcock; One plaiting machine, by ditto; Hydraulic cloth press by Haighton and Helm; One cop winding engine of 204 spindles by Wilkinson; One ditto of 164 spindles by same maker; Three beaming frames with patent stopping motion by Howard and Bullough; About 500 sets of healds and reeds, 44s and 60s; A large quantity of shuttles, strapping, change wheels, spare looms and back beams, weft and waste cans, warping bobbins etc.; One eight day clock, grindstone in iron frame, dry gas meter, water meter, tacklers benches, vices and tools, several pairs of scales and weights, two platform weighing machines, oil cisterns, heald racks, cloth tables, twisting and looming frames, one capital tape sizing machine with 66 inch and 48 inch cylinders, with pipes taps wood covering trunks etc; Also, steam engine attached to the tape machine for the purpose of working it when the other machine is standing; Large mixing apparatus with four agitators including the pipes and taps etc; Capital yarn tester by Goodbrand and Holland; Wrap reel by Elce, with scales and weights; Excellent office desk with bay wood top and ten drawers; Beam truck, beam rack, hoist rope brushes, oil cans, oil bottles and many other sundry articles.
>
> For further information and to view apply to the Auctioneer at his office, 53 Manchester Road, Burnley from whom printed catalogues may be had on and after 3 January. The sale to commence at 11 o'clock in the forenoon.

NEWTOWN MILL

This mill is on Vulcan Street, off Cow Lane, on what is now named Lodge Square, but formerly it was Kay Street. I know, it can get confusing! The Newtown Mill, not to be confused with Newtown Steel Works, was built in 1864 (see date stone). Notice too the fine arched windows on either side of the present-day main entrance, but which was formerly the engine house, also, a now scarce cobble court at the right and rear of the building. The mill chimney attached to Newtown Mill, now cleaned, is one of the finest remaining in Burnley. In the 1890s, the Newtown Mill also operated across from the present-day building, on the site of what was to become later the Empire Theatre and Cinema. It was this mill that was operated by the Tunstill Brothers in 1865; they also worked the Goodham Mill and a mill at Brierfield. Harling, Harling and Todd, cotton spinners and manufacturers, were working the Newtown Mill in 1868; they were perhaps better known for their involvement with making looms. The Newtown Mill was used as a lodging house for thirty odd years from after the First World War until around 1948, and from about 1990 it became Lodge House, and is now used as offices.

Northbridge Mill.

NORTH BRIDGE MILL (HURTLEY'S), ELM STREET, BURNLEY

John Hurtley and Son, cotton spinners and manufacturers, were working the North Bridge Mill in 1868 and in 1879, and it dates from around this time. John retired the following year and lived at the large Wilfield House which used to stand on Padiham Road near to the Barracks railway station. John was born at Settle in Yorkshire about 1807 and lived at Wilfield House with his daughter Elizabeth. Also in 1879, William Bancroft and Co. Ltd worked at part of the mill, through to about 1923. William employed sixty-seven operatives and 228 looms in the 1880s and lived at No. 25 Palatine Square. In the mid-1940s, John Walton and Son Ltd, cotton manufacturers, were operating at the mill. The mill is now part of the North Bridge Complex – a small commercial unit. North Bridge Mill consists of a three-storey sandstone spinning mill, with a smaller four-storey apex section. Modern additions are to the rear, with a small weaving shed and warehousing on the Daneshouse Road side. The weaving shed is shown as New Hall Mill on a map for 1912, this is in addition to the other New Hall Mill further up Elm Street.

OAKBANK MILL (OR OAK BANK), CASTERTON AVENUE, BURNLEY

Worked by Ormerod Whitaker, and Sons Ltd (1901). In 1945 they were running 1,080 looms. The firm was founded by Ormerod Whitaker and his sons John Ormerod and James – they built Oak Bank Mill eleven years after commencing business at Rake Head Mill. The son, John Ormerod Whitaker of 'Highfield' Briercliffe Road, died in April 1949. For over forty years he was a member of the Manchester Cotton Exchange. The mill was built in 1913, and closed down in 1958, as a cotton mill. It was taken over shortly afterwards by Eric Cowpe and named 'Diana Cowpe', after his daughter – do you remember the candlewick bedstead covers made here? At its peak over 18,000 bedspreads were being manufactured here each week, more than half of them going as exports, to nearly forty countries. A factory shop also sold a wide range of soft furnishings, duvet covers, pillowcases and curtaining. The mill still survives, but its future is uncertain and it is not in operation at the time of writing.

OAK MOUNT MILL, WISEMAN STREET, BURNLEY

The mill was colloquially known as Wiseman Street Mill. The Oak Mount Mill still survives to this day, but on the map of 1910 is marked 'disused'. The mill was built in three stages; the weaving shed next to the three-storey warehouse was built prior to 1850, and shows up on a map of 1851. This may have been built by William Hopwood who in 1843 was listed as cotton manufacturer, of Hopwood Street Westgate. The lower two storeys of the warehouse were built in 1887, and the top floor was built in 1905. The single-storey office block nearest to the street was built in 1910.

The very first mill around here was built in, or about, 1830, as a woollen mill, but this was destroyed by fire. Where the lower car park is today used to be a 'mill pond', now filled in. The writer remembers this pond as being part of Massey's Brewery, or at least it was often full of their old barrels with which he made rafts to sail on the pond with as a lad. The steam engine that drove the machinery at Oak Mount Mill remains in situ, and hopes are entertained this will soon become a tourist attraction. The chimney too is worth a mention, one of the finest still standing in Burnley, an impressive structure over 120ft high. The 'yard' above the mill on the right-hand side near the canal also had building used in connection with Oak Mount Mill, but these have been demolished, after being gutted by fire in 1884. A fine arch in the perimeter wall on the canalside can still be seen, in-filled with a rubble wall.

The Oak Mount Mill belonged to Christopher Bracewell in the 1880s and consisted of a five-storey spinning mill It was opened on 2 September 1875, and contained 30,000 spindles. It consisted of two wings, which stood at right angles to each other, one facing north, the other facing east. This is the mill besides the canal, which was destroyed by fire in 1884. The fire broke out on Friday 28 March, at around ten minutes to ten, and was thought to have been caused through friction on one of the wheels. Besides the town fire brigade, the military brigade from Clifton Barracks were also soon on the scene. After about an hour the roof of the mill caved in, and it was soon evident that it couldn't be saved. Soon the gable end came down with such force that it drove the canal tow path and banking into the water. It was stated that the alarm was given by a man named J. Turner through the 'Trafalgar telegraph station'. Turner was employed erecting a tall chimney for Massey's (Victoria) Mill when he saw the outbreak. The total damage was put at some £30,000. By 1923, the Oak Mount Mill was in the occupation of Major Greenwood and was a cotton-waste shop.

OLD HALL MILL, OLD HALL STREET, BURNLEY

The Old Hall Mill bears the name and date '1902' on the canal side of the mill. The building, a spinning mill, is of three storeys – stone-built – and survives adjacent to Old Hall Canal Bridge.

Old Hall Mill.

The date stone of Old Hall Mill.

OLIVE MOUNT MILL, JUNCTION STREET, BURNLEY

The Olive Mount Mill was opened in 1863 by Messrs Hopwood's (in 1861, according to Walter Bennett's *History of Burnley*). In 1868 it was being worked by Stansfield and Maden, cotton spinners and manufacturers, probably under lease from Hopwood's. The Olive Mount Mill was on Junction Street in the Whittlefield District of Burnley, beyond the Junction Street Mill, a former Corn Mill, and the old coal staith belonging to the former Whittlefield Colliery on Junction Street. There are no remains of Olive Mount Mill; the site of the former mill now lies under the embankment of the M65 Motorway.

The mill suffered in a number of fires over the years, such as the one in December 1927, when the mill 'went up like a furnace'. The final demise of the mill probably came in another fierce blaze that took place in February 1959. The mill at this time was being worked by Robert Pickles, and consisted of a three-storey block containing canteen, toilets, repair works – all of which were completely gutted in the blaze. The following morning little was left of this part of the mill, save for the gaunt 60ft mill chimney standing in the middle of the site as if in defiance to the destructive blaze. At the outbreak of the Second World War, the mill was being run by The Olive Mount Mill Co., and was running 800 looms, making satteens, jeans and twills.

OXFORD MILL, OXFORD ROAD, BURNLEY

The Oxford Mill still stands on the corner of Oxford Road and Parliament Street, and was built as a spinning and weaving shed in 1874. (However, a report on the fire there in 1946, states that the mill was built in 1854). The original mill was four storeys high, with a water tower at the Todmorden Road end six storeys high. The Oxford Mill (1920) Ltd, cotton manufacturers, were working the mill in 1923, and it had a floor space of 6,180 yards, and a site area of 4,332 yards. The latter firm still had the mill in 1934, as a spinning and weaving shed with 578 looms, but it was 'stopped and unoccupied'.

Among the amenities offered when the mill was put up for let in 1935, were 'hoists, electric lights with generator, automatic sprinkler with water tower, fireproof doors, fire escapes, and shafting throughout the main mill'. Water for the one Lancashire boiler (new in 1913) was obtained from the River Calder by right of agreement. The boiler, fitted with Proctor's stokers and Green's economiser, provided the power for the 700hp Cross Compound Condensing Steam Engine, fitted with rope flywheel. Simpson and Co., cotton-waste merchants, were occupying the mill in the mid-1940s.

A large part of Oxford Mill was gutted in a spectacular blaze in November 1946; three firemen were injured in the blaze which cost around £20,000 in damages. The property at this time was owned by James Dixon and was sub-divided into parts occupied by Simpson and Co. Waste Dealers, Burnley Appliance Co., Granville Storage Ltd, and East Lancashire Platers. There was worse to come: in June the following year the mill claimed two lives while undergoing demolition following the fire in the previous November. They were named as being George O'Connor, aged forty, of St Stephen's Street, Burnley and Edward Rothwell, aged forty, of Heywood Street, Great Harwood.

Oxford Mill.

PARK SHED, LEYLAND ROAD, BURNLEY

Worked by James Foulds and Sons, in 1923, 'Parkshed', (as it is spelt on the date stone), was built in 1907 and was claimed by many as being the last cotton mill built in Burnley. The building, which survived until late 2005, was of brick and stone structure, with slate roof, and towers either side. At the time of writing the site of the old mill is being transformed into new housing. James Foulds had almost 900 looms stopped during a depression in the cotton trade of the 1920s and '30s. Part of Park Shed at this time was also being run by Sharp Thornber and Sons; indeed it was built by James Foulds and Sharp Thornber and divided into two sections, one for each to work. Sharp Thornber was born in 1858, the son of James and Ann Thornber, who at one time lived at No. 135 Westgate. Later Sharp went on to live at Powell Street near Scotts Park – he died in 1933. It was said that the miners working at the old Bee Hole Colliery near Brunshaw Bottom could hear the weavers at work, while they toiled underground getting the coal.

PARKER LANE MILL

Parker Lane Mill was a mill dating from around 1845, obviously on Parker Lane, and one which closed around 1869. Unfortunately, little else is known.

PARSONAGE MILL, KEIGHLEY GREEN, BURNLEY

This mill occupied the land around the rear of the Church Street car park, or the present-day St Peter's Centre. A Christopher Hartley is listed as a cotton manufacturer at Keighley Green in 1818 through to 1824, but it was John Moore who probably built the mill around 1830, on the site of the old parsonage. This old parsonage was, according to a correspondent in the *Burnley Express* on 9 May 1874, 'originally surrounded by ancient trees and beautiful walks... but the house had been untenanted for many years. It is now [1874] being demolished to make room for a warehouse for Mr Smallpage at Parsonage Mill'. It was also pointed out when the mill was built, that there had been an ancient right of way over stepping-stones across the Brun at the bottom of Rakefoot, by a pathway. The owners of the Mill replied that the pathway had been closed with the consent of the landlord to whom they had paid compensation, and that it was dangerous for their workers, particularly the children, to cross the stepping stones. Nevertheless they offered to give land for the building of a bridge. This later became known as the 'Police Bridge', which many will recall, so named on account of its use by the policemen going to Keighley Green police station, which took over the Keighley Green Chapel in 1867.

Isaiah Smallpage, cotton spinner and manufacturer, lived at Palatine Square and employed 270 hands. Messrs Spencer and Moore, cotton spinners and manufacturers, were working the Parsonage Mills both in 1848 and in 1868. In 1879, it was being leased to the Kershaw Brothers. Earlier, in the 1840s, Spencer and Moore were also cotton manufacturers on Croft Street. The Parsonage Mill was built principally as a woollen factory, but later used for weaving, and in its latter days both weaving and spinning. The Parsonage Mill was up for sale by auction in March 1897. At this time it had a floor space of 1,830 square yards, and a 'McNaughted' Beam Engine of 600hp, with three pinion wheels and three second motion shafts. The mill at this time belonged to the late Isaiah Smallpage. Mr Smallpage had died in July 1880. The mill was demolished, at least in part, in 1933, although for many years the site was occupied as a scrap-metal merchants (Woodfield and Turners?). In 1955, Anderson's Printers used a part of the offices belonging to the old Parsonage Mill near the Keighley Green entrance to the Police Bridge, and directly across from their premises was Thomas Rigg's blacksmith shop. There are no remains today of this historic mill, all the area has been developed. The Parsonage Mill has a difficult history to follow: the mill was extended and pulled down over the years, and was also known by different names.

PEEL MILL, GANNOW LANE, BURNLEY

This is the mill just over the canal bridge on Gannow Lane on the left-hand side coming down from Gannow Top. Peel Mill probably dates from 1896, when the new steam engine there was started – it was built by George Walmsley. The mill was in fact being worked by George Walmsley and Sons Ltd in 1945, who were operating 2,062 looms, and it still survives today as 'Cloverbrook'. Part of the work done here at Cloverbrook was the dyeing and finishing of cloth manufactured at Riverside Knitting at Lune Street, in Padiham. The process though caused a number of complaints about the terrible smell it created, particularly in the year 1996, and the company was served with a notice to reduce the smell. George Walmsley, the mill owner at Peel Mill was the son of John Walmsley, a cotton manufacturer who worked the Hargher Wood Mill, and was born in Burnley around 1852. On 6 October 1875, George, then living at South Parade (the old name for Manchester Road above the canal bridge), married Miss Thirza Eva Peel at the Union Chapel Blackpool. Peel Mill in fact takes it name from George's wife's maiden name: one of their children was also named Leonard Peel Walmsley to mark this fact. This was common practice at this time, especially when there was no male line in the family – it simply kept the name of the bride's family going. George and his wife continued to live at Manchester Road for a number of years, and even had a spell at Tarleton House on Todmorden Road, before moving to St Anne's near Blackpool. It was here in January 1918 that George Walmsley, the former Burnley cotton manufacturer, passed away.

The son Leonard Peel Walmsley had entered the family business at Peel Mill, with his elder brother Frank, and unfortunately came to an untimely end in 1924. Leonard lived at St Anne's with his two unmarried sisters – the house here was actually named 'Tarleton' in recollection of their former Burnley home. Leonard tended to the Manchester side of the mill business, returning to St Anne's each weekend. He had served in the army during the First World War during the years 1915 to 1918 and reached the rank of captain – but was badly gassed during 1918 and was invalided out of the forces. Strong light, such as sunlight, would often have an effect on his eyesight as a result of the gassing, and it was thought that this might have contributed to his death. Leonard was on business in Manchester in April 1924 on Upper Chorlton Road when he spotted a tram which would take him to the city office. He stepped out into the road to indicate that he wanted to tram to stop for him and he was hit by a heavy lorry – death was almost instantaneous. Leonard was brought back to Burnley and buried at the municipal cemetery. Six employees of the firm George Walmsley and Sons acted as bearers, and besides the immediate family there was also a large number of the workmen and women at the graveside. Floral tributes were many, and included one from the Peel Mill Football Club – Leonard was clearly well liked as a mill owner and an employer.

Before leaving Peel Mill look for the iron door at the corner of the mill where you entersthe mill yard. A ginny track, or a small mineral railway, running from the Smallshaw Sidings belonging to the Exors of John Hargreaves, the local colliery owners, once ran right through

Peel Mill.

the side of the Peel Mill here, in a tunnel to a canal side coal depot. This indicates that the ginny track was there before the mill.

PEEL'S MILL, SANDYGATE, BURNLEY

Peel's Mill used to occupy the site now taken by the former Dexter's Paint shop at the bottom end of Sandygate, and dated from around 1790. The Peels, who ran the mill, were connected with Sir Robert Peel, and this was the first mill in Burnley to be run by a steam engine. A rate book of 1801 shows Jonathan Peel, a relative of Sir Robert Peel, as occupying a house and garden near the 'club houses': we are also informed that Sir Robert was a frequent visitor. Elizabeth Peel, who belonged to the family of the Peels of Bridge End and Lowerhouse, on her deathbed in 1800, left the sum of £1,241 15s, to be distributed among the poor of Habergham Eaves and Burnley in such a way as the trustees should direct. This became known as 'Miss Peel's Charity', which I believe still exists. The Peel's Mill, however, burnt down in 1798, and remained a blackened ruin for many years afterwards. History they say repeats itself, and today we have a similar blackened ruin, and not far away in the form of Slater's Clock Tower Mill. In later years when Hindle Rawcliffe built houses and shops in this area, the cellars of those houses were large, strongly built, and capacious: being in fact adaptations of the cellars at the old mill. The Peel family were also connected with the cotton printing trade at Caldervale Print Works'. A directory for the year 1792 says that:

> Messrs Peel, Yate and Co. have erected two large buildings here, viz., one for the engravers, print-cutters, and calico printers, the other for spinning of cotton by machines, with dyehouse

and bleaching croft. Messrs Peel, Ashworth, Cockshutt, Heeles, and Alsop, all from Bolton-le-Moors have warehouses here, and employ great numbers of weavers and spinners in the cotton branch of all ages and both sexes, who earn a competent livelihood.

PENDLE VIEW SHED, JUNCTION STREET, BURNLEY

The Pendle View Mill was being worked in 1879 by Francis Amos and James Holdsworth, probably on a 'room and power' basis, although for many years later by Robert Pickles Ltd. The mill dated from around 1865. The site is now destroyed, and only perimeter walls survive at the time of writing. Pendle View Shed was the last mill on the left on Junction Street, just before the canal. It was stated in 1934 that this mill, run by Nuttall and Crook, had almost 600 looms, but 'had never been started since a fire some years ago'. This was the fire that took place in January 1928, when damage was caused to the value of an estimated £20,000. The mill at this time had 584 looms, and around 200 mill operatives were put out of work. The fire took hold in a three-storey section of the mill, the ground floor of which housed the engine and boilers, the second floor the winding and beaming room, and the next floor the taping room. The whole of the roof collapsed in the inferno. Rather like the Phoenix, the mill rose from the ashes, and in the 1940s was once again being worked by Robert Pickles.

PENTRIDGE MILL, HOLMES STREET, BURNLEY

The mill still survives, (albeit in a rather shoddy fashion), as various industrial units, part of which was converted into the Pentridge Cinema in 1910. The Fulledge Manufacturing Co. were working on the Holmes Street mill in 1914. Pentridge Mill dated from around 1860, and finished manufacturing cotton around 1965. The mill had 33, 260 spindles in the mid-1880s.

PICKUP CROFT MILL, PICKUP CROFT, BURNLEY

This mill, originally a corn mill was at the top of Basket Street near the 'culvert'. It became a spinning mill in 1846 till around 1873, and Robert Briggs is listed as working the Pickup Croft Mill in 1865. 'A fall off in demand brought financial difficulties to the owners of Pickup Croft Mill in 1858'. Nothing remains of this mill – the site being redeveloped long since. The *Burnley Advertiser* for 27 February 1858 contained the following advert:

Valuable Mill Machinery and Premises for Sale in Burnley. To be sold by Auction by Messrs C. Denbigh and Son at the Thorn Inn, in Burnley, in the County of Lancashire on Monday the 15th. Day of March 1858 at seven o'clock in the evening, subject to the conditions as will be there produced. All that valuable Cotton Mill, or Factory situated in Burnley in the occupation of James and Nathan Smallpage, and called by the name of Pickup Croft Mill, together with the scutching house, boiler house, chimney, engine house, gig house, office, smithy, warehouse, and other buildings, steam engine, vacant land and yards thereto adjoining and belonging, steam pipes, boilers, shafting, gearing, and all the other landlord fixtures and appendages. Also, one half of the street, 8 yards wide adjoining to the said mill and premises

A view of Basket Street. (courtesy of the Briercliffe Society)

called Basket Street. The engine is of 30hp, the machinery chiefly consists of four pair of self acting mules, 4.800 spindles, 8 sets of counter shafts and pulleys, 8 drums, 4 warping mills, 3 winding engines, 600 spindles, 8 roving frames, 928 spindles, 4 slubbing frames etc. The mill is 5 stories high, and 43 yards long by 12 yards wide. The property is situated near the centre of town, and is bounded southwards by the banks of the Leeds Liverpool Canal, eastwards by the said street of 8 yards wide, and westward by Pilling Street. The property is lease-hold for a term of 930 years, and commenced on 11th. August 1825. The whole is subject to ground rent amounting to £22.14s.9d. For further particulars apply to Messrs Alcock and Holmes, solicitors, Burnley.

PILLINGFIELD MILL, AQUEDUCT STREET, BURNLEY

This mill was of some antiquity, being run in the late 1840s by Smallpage and Lord. The Pillingfield Mill at one time had 40,000 spindles, and was worked by Brown and Spencer; the Halsam's; Webster Fishwick and others over the years. Between 1890 and 1892, the Pillingfield Mill was purchased by the Corporation, who built the town's electricity station, the supply of which was inaugurated on 22 August 1893. The former mill site is now taken over by car parking space, and another mill much nearer the 'culvert', also known as Pillingfield, was marked as being a corn mill on a map of 1910. The Pillingfield cotton mill was almost besides the River Calder

Primrose Mill, Harle Syke, after the fire in April 1921.

near where it flows under the canal, and shows up clearly on the map for the year 1851. There are no remains of the former Pillingfield Mill.

PLUMBE STREET SHED, PLUMBE STREET, BURNLEY

The mill was worked by the Whitham Brothers, and was in fact always known locally as 'Whitham's' Mill'. The mill, a cotton-weaving shed, was finished around 1959, and the shed itself was demolished around 1985. The surrounding walls of the weaving shed still survive, as does the main office block; now used by other industries. The mill is at the top end of Plumbe Street on the right-hand side just before Parliament Street. In March 1938, James Lord of Emily Street retired after thirty-seven years service at the mill. The mill workers presented him with a radio set to mark his retirement.

PRIMROSE MILL, MARTIN STREET, BURNLEY

The Primrose Mill is still with us, a fine and typical weaving shed. Richard Stuttard was working this and the nearby Byerden Mill in the mid-1920s. It was worked in the mid-1940s by a number of firms such as J. H. Crowther Ltd (cotton and rayon) manufacturers; Frank Atkinson; Villiers Street Manufacturing Co. Ltd and others. The mill bears two dates: '1903' (of the original building) and, on a lintel, '1912'. *The Burnley Express* of 5 May 1937 stated that:

> Miss Burnley for 1937–38 will be Miss Janey Tomlinson of 4 Whalley Street who has been selected by readers of the 'Daily Dispatch' in the ballot competition. Miss Tomlinson who is 19

years of age is employed at the Primrose Mill of Messrs R. Stuttard Ltd and our photographer found her busy at her looms shortly after her success was published last Monday morning.

Over forty years later, in April 1979, Janey Roland brought back her memories of being a former cotton queen when she visited the Weaver's Triangle Visitors Centre on Manchester Road. 'It was a glorious year', she said in 1937 when she left the weaving shed to open exhibitions and garden centres and visit other mills. During her reign she visited the Chorley Exhibition, met Lord Shuttleworth of Gawthorpe Hall, and opened a garden party there. Back then Janey lived with her parents in Whalley Street, but in 1979 she had exchanged her looms for a part-time job helping out with school dinners at Casterton Avenue Primary School. By 1990 Janey had become Mrs Janey Smith. A photograph accompanied the above 1937 article which will be of interest for Tomlinson family history researchers.

PRIMROSE MILL, HARRISON STREET, HARLE SYKE

The Primrose Mill was begun in 1905 by William West – formerly of Simpson and West, cotton manufacturers of Harle Syke Mill – and was to contain 1,050 looms: it opened in January 1906. William West was born in Briercliffe, and twenty-one years previous to Primrose Mill opening, William was just a cotton loom jobber living at Haggate with his wife Elizabeth. The mill engine here at Primrose Mill was actually named 'Elizabeth West' after William's wife. 'Elizabeth West' was sadly scrapped in January 1976 when Crowthers, the mill owners at that time, decided to sell up. It was by the 1920s that the Primrose Mill was being worked on the 'room and power system' and occupied by four other firms, which included Messrs Crowther, Messrs Atkinson, The Limefield Manufacturing Co. and the Queen Street Manufacturing Co. The preparation department at Primrose Mill was a two-storey building with a floor space of around 2,500sq ft, and adjoining this was a warehouse. At the rear was a large weaving shed containing around 1,000 looms.

There was a serious fire at the mill in April 1921 that broke out in the preparation department near the engine house. The mill did recover however, having been completely rebuilt in the same style, and was being worked by Frank Atkinson Ltd in the 1940s, with 795 looms in operation, manufacturing printers, satteens, cambrics, limbrics, warp satins and jeans. Frank Atkinson the mill owner lived at Cockden House at Briercliffe. Another fire in July 2005 caused a great deal of damage when the mill was occupied by the firm of bed and furniture manufacturers 'Sweet Dream'. Flames as high as 50ft rose into the night air and caused neighbouring houses to shake – the blaze, it was said, could be seen at Accrington, almost six miles away. This spelt the end of Primrose Mill and it was demolished shortly afterwards.

The Primrose Mill was a stone-built weaving shed with a stub red-brick chimney. The fine engine house here had some nice stonework, and the two-storey frontage contained the warehousing was used as part of the mill shop. A typical northern light roof was to the rear and a cast-iron water tank.

QUEEN STREET MILL, QUEEN STREET, BURNLEY

This building which still survives was built some time prior to 1848, as Queen Street Mill, a cotton-weaving mill; it shows up on the map for 1851. In 1887 William Bracewell was running 1,078 looms at this and the George Street Sheds. It later became an engineering shop, but following a fire in 1916, the mill was restored to its former use, being renamed Charlotte Street Mill. Today, Charlotte Street Mill is occupied by a number of small units, such as a plumbers' supply works, and a bike shop. The gable building at the end nearest to the Newtown Steel Works has a fine cast-iron lintel with the date '1882'. At the other side of the mill, facing the footbridge coming from Trafalgar, there is a loading bay door with a block and tackle attachment on the girder above.

QUEEN STREET MILL, QUEEN STREET, HARLE SYKE

This was a steam-powered weaving shed, built in 1894/5 not by great capitalists or mill owners, but as a village co-operative. When the mill was opened, two enthusiastic members of a local brass band climbed the mill chimney, and one of them played a cornet solo from the top. Queen Street Mill, with its steam engine and machinery intact, is a unique survivor out of the many hundreds of textile mills in Lancashire.

The mill today is the home of the Museum of the Lancashire Textiles Industry, the 500hp steam engine 'Peace' drives the shed and the looms, and weaving is carried out whenever the mill is open. Here the visitor can experience just what it was like to work in a weaving shed typical of Victorian times complete with the noise of 300 power looms. Theme days are held at various times aimed especially at the children to show what factory life was like – there are even Victorian classrooms and displays of Victorian toys. While the children are being entertained the parents can browse around the extensive mill shop with goods on display which were made from cloth woven at Queen Street Mill, or simply take things easy and have a cup of tea. The Queen Street Mill was worked by the Queen Street Manufacturing Co. Ltd 1945, and designed as a stone-built single-storey weaving shed with warehouse attached. The red-brick chimney bears the words 'Queen Street Mill'. The fine boiler room and engine room here deserves observation besides the mill lodge. The Queen Street Manufacturing Co. Ltd (1894) were running 1,040 looms here in 1940, Willie Burrows was the mill secretary and lived at No. 30 Queen Street, and Joe Sutcliffe was the salesman.

QUEEN'S MILL, NEW HALL STREET

This mill still survives, being built in 1887, and opened on 19 April that year. The mill eventually had 857 looms, and was worked and built by John Spencer (Burnley) Ltd who is listed working the mill both in 1923, and in 1945. The building today consists of a two-storey stone-built spinning mill/warehouse with weaving shed to rear. A fine engine/boiler house has arched windows with stub of former mill chimney. An old employee at Queen's Mill was Ada Kippax of New Hall Street, who started with the Spencers' at the age of ten years, when the firm had their looms on Elm Street. In 1930, she was the only employee who could remember the opening of the Queen's Mill at the age of sixty-four, and she was still able to run four looms. The Spencer's treated their workers with some respect, and to mark the jubilee of the Queen's Mill they took all the workers from the Queen's Mill and their Imperial Mill at Rosegrove to Blackpool. About 800 workers left the town on two special trains, and when they arrived they were treated to tea and provided with free admission to the Winter Gardens there – how many firms do that today?

Queen Street Mill, Harle Syke.

Queen's Mill, Newhall Street.

QUEENSGATE MILL (HALSTEAD'S), HIND STREET, BURNLEY

This mill was worked by Edmund Halstead from 1903 right up to 1962, and possibly beyond. The weaving shed part of Queensgate Mill was demolished around 1951, and NorWeb took over part of the complex as offices. The walls of the former mill still survive, enclosing Dove Court Residential Nursing Home, although the mill itself has been demolished and completely disappeared. The mill dated from 1903 and was always known locally as 'Halstead's' from the firm of Edmund Halstead Ltd (1903).

At the start of the Second World War the firm was running 1,607 looms, manufacturing jeans, twills coloured goods and shirting. Edmund Halstead was a fine example of a self-made man. He started off in the cotton trade at Bishop House Mill in 1892 before building the Queensgate Mill in 1906. One of his main interests though was the Burnley Victoria Hospital, and for twenty-nine years he was on the board of management. He was chairman here for seventeen years, as well as being a trustee. Edmund was also a county magistrate and a trustee of the Mechanic's Institute at Burnley, and a commissioner for taxes for twenty years, as well as being a member of the town council. As a manufacturer he gained great wealth, and was able to travel widely and live at the fine house at No. 319 Colne Road named 'Rokeby'; it was here that Edmund died at the grand age of eighty-seven years, in August 1947.

RAKE HEAD MILL, BISHOP STREET, BURNLEY

The Rake Head Mill dates from before 1843, when John and William Brennand were cotton spinners and manufacturers at Rake Head mill, but by 1848 it was John Brennand and Brothers who were working the mill. The mill appears on the first edition map for 1844–48. The mill was up for sale by auction in March 1871, following the voluntary liquidation of John Brennand, and was described as follows:

> Machinery, Stores and other effects, in that part of the above named premises, lately occupied by Mr. John Brennand consisting of 236 power looms all in really first class working condition and fit up with templates &c complete. 139 of which 45 inch reed space by Wilkinson, 96 of 40 inch reed space by Wilkinson, and 21 of 45 inch reed space by Bracewell and Bullock. A plaiting machine by Graham and Sons, a cop winding machine of 180 spindles by Harling and Todd, and five beaming frames by Harrison…[also] to be let, Room and Power on the above named premises for 256 looms with ample warehousing and convenience for Tape Sizing.

The mill was evidently bought by John Clegg for by 1879, the Rakehead Mill was being worked by him with 322 looms. However, in 1887 the mill was being worked by John Grey with 1,104 looms and in June 1887, it was stated that the 'Burnley Lane Self-Help Society' had raised £2,000 and installed 420 looms at the Rake Head Mill recently vacated by Grey Brothers. The difficulties proved too great and soon the company went into liquidation. The Rake Head Mill was being worked by Emeleas Manufacturing Co. Ltd in 1945, and Sutcliffes (Burnley) Ltd. The site has now been taken by the developments that include the Quik-Save Store and other retail outlets.

There are no remains of the former Rake Head Mill: it was demolished in November 1993, and was last used by 'Dorma'. Local historian James Howell said, at the time of demolition, that the first mill on that land was known as the 'Moorfield site' and was converted from a building that served as the town's first workhouse from 1731 to 1785. The conversion was done about 1820 by John Brennand, who was the first occupant of Byerden House, now a Socialist club. The family gave its name to nearby Brennand Street. In the mid-1830s the former workhouse building was demolished, and a purpose-built mill was erected – it was to become one of the most important mills in the town. Part of the mill was destroyed in a fire in 1870, after which the Brennand's went into liquidation. Following this, other manufacturers have included William Rawlinson in the 1880s. In the twentieth century Whitehead and Leaver occupied Rakehead Mill for twenty years and Ernest Foster occupied part of it in the 1930s and '40s. Dorma occupied the mill in its latter years, and what later became the firm's car park was once a large mill lodge, which was popular with anglers within living memory. The lodge (actually two lodges) were located at the bottom (Brennand Street) end. A massive boiler explosion at the Rake Head Mill in the 1870s killed two men, Michael Maloy and George Smith Johnson.

Seventy-two years of constant employment in the cotton industry was the proud record and claim of eighty-two year old James Chadwick of Ross Street in Brierfield in January 1945. He celebrated his eighty-second birthday at Rake Head Mill by putting in another full day's weaving. James was believed to be the oldest working weaver in the area at that time. He would rise every working day at 5.30 a.m., have a little breakfast and then catch the bus to work to run four looms. James, the eldest of nine children, began work in a joiner's shop aged nine years, for the sum of 1s 6d a week. Twelve months later he went acting as a tenter for his mother, and except for a brief period when he worked as a tackler he had been weaving ever since. Mr Chadwick had no recipe to offer for his longevity or his fitness for a man of his age – and he would not go as far as saying that having been a bachelor added years to his life. He still enjoyed a pint at the Brierfield Liberal Club each night and a puff of his tobacco pipe.

RISHTON MILL, GUNSMITH LANE, BURNLEY

The Rishton Mill was besides the 'Culvert' on Gunsmith Lane, now part of Yorkshire Street on the left-hand side going towards Turf Moor. The mill was worked and built by the Folds, on land bought off the Hitchon's, and was built as a spinning mill. The main building consisted of three floors, with a floor space of 4,800 yards, and a store of two floors with 450 yards of floor space. James and Obadiah Folds ran the mill in 1845, after embarking on the business of cotton spinning, the large house built on site by the Folds later became the Star Inn. By 1887 the Folds had a total of 29,803 spindles running here and at Trafalgar Shed. A timber yard is marked on the place occupied by Rishton Mill in 1827, although the mill does show up on a map for the year 1851. A prominent feature at the mill was the square tower that stood in the middle, protruding from the main building with a castle-type parapet on top. James Folds was also mayor of Burnley in 1866. In 1934, the Rishton Mill was occupied by 'several firm engaged in various businesses'. Demolition was begun at Rishton Mill in that year, 1934, when the chimney was dropped, and in 1936, the whole structure was demolished. Later the Odeon Cinema was built on the site, and later still the first Sainsbury Store. Gunsmith Lane, is the address for the Rishton Mill and probably takes its name from John Stirling, who was a 'gun maker' here in 1845.

Rishton Mill. (courtesy of the Briercliffe Society)

ROBERT'S MILL

This is apparently another name for the Market Bridge Mill, River Street, Burnley. In South Parade, the old name for Manchester Road above the canal, Robert's Mill stood near the canal bridge.

ROSEGROVE MILL, GANNOW LANE, BURNLEY

This mill, on Gannow Lane, was worked by Nuttall and Crook Ltd 1945, or 'Nuts and Crucks' as it was called locally. Nuttall and Crook's closed in February 1960. At one time the firm was running 25,000 spindles and 1,638 looms. In February 1964, the mill was entirely destroyed in a spectacular fire when owned by C.K.S. Engineering. Temple and Sutcliffe were listed as working the Rosegrove Mills in 1865, and it probably dated from around that time. James Temple, one of the partners, was born in Norden in Yorkshire, and under Temple and Sutcliffe the firm employed 308 hands at the Rosegrove Mill. James married Mary Ann Sutcliffe (hence the name of the firm) in 1854 at St John's the Divine at Cliviger. The mill was on the right-hand side of Gannow Lane after going over the canal bridge going towards Rosegrove. It must have been a proud day in April 1949 when the whole of the mill was stopped to give William Lord, who had been employed at the mill for nearly fifty years, his retirement present. Thomas Nuttall, the director of the firm, presented Mr

Lord with a money gift on behalf of the staff at the mill. Thomas began at the mill in 1898 when it was being run by Temple and Sutcliffe, working as a warehouseman, and was still there when Nuttall and Crook took over the mill in 1916. Thomas first started work doing part-time work in the mills at the age of ten years – working at filling the twists for the winders at Walmsley's Shed in Canning Street, he then spent a number of years working at their Woodfield Mill, and then three years at Berry's Shed at Whittlefield before eventually going and settling down at Rosegrove Mill.

ROYLE ROAD MILL

This mill was evidently in existence in 1848 on Royle Road and was worked by John Walker and Company, but nothing else is known. It appears in a directory for the year 1848.

ST JAMES'S ROW MILL

St James's Row exists today off St James's Street, and there was apparently a mill here dating from around 1815 and which ran until around 1830. The mill was a jenny spinning mill and was erected by Thomas Kay. There are no remains of St James's Row Mill.

SALFORD MILL, ROYLE ROAD, BURNLEY

The Salford Mill used to stand directly in front of the present-day Town Mouse pub, which was formerly the Salford Hotel. The mill was evidently of some age, being built in 1821 as a cotton spinning and weaving factory by John Eltoft. A building is marked here on Fishwick's Map of 1827; certainly the mill was there in 1851. It appears that Eltoft leased the mill out to Edward Pollard, who was listed as being a cotton spinner and manufacturer at Salford mill in 1843. The mill remained in the hands of the Eltoft's until 1859, when it was taken over by J and M. Kippax, cotton spinners and manufacturers. The building consisted of three blocks, two of which surrounded a small spinning mill, which housed 6,000 spindles along with a scutching room and engine house. The main block was four storeys high, with an attic room on top. Here, on the ground floor was a carding room with twenty-four carding engines: the rest was taken up by mule spindles, around 20,000 in total. It was also here, in 1893, that a policeman named George Henry Lockwood was killed when a portion of the building collapsed on him while fighting a fire.

For many years the Salford Mill was used by the Co-operative Wholesale Warehouse, which might have had something to do with the building of the Leo Store in later years. In fact it was purchased by the Co-op as far back as 1893, the year of the fire mentioned above. Here, in later years, battery operated milk floats would come in every morning to be recharged in a room at the back of the mill. The door was often left open, and it was too much of a temptation for the younger lads. As a child I spent many a happy hour riding up and down the cobbled Bankhouse Street on the battery operated milk floats with long handles at the front to steer by, until chased off by the caretaker (This may have been another name for the Bankhouse Mill mentioned previously).

Salford Mill.

SANDYGATE MILL, SANDYGATE, BURNLEY

According to most sources and tradition, the Sandygate Mill was begun in 1858–59 by George Slater, of the Clock Tower Mill; however a mill shows up on this site on the map of 1851. The engine house and chimney are located in the near by Slater Terrace. Originally, the mill included, as well as the present weaving mill, a spinning shed. The Sandygate Mill was completely built by 1862, and was three-storeys high, with a later addition in the roof space, giving another floor in the middle. The mill was last occupied by Lords Printers, and was burnt out a few years ago. It survives at the time of writing, albeit in a blackened state. Blakey and Nephews Ltd worked both the Sandygate and Gannow Sheds in 1923, and were also the owners of the Sandygate Mill. The Sandygate Mill Co Ltd worked the mill, in 1945. Built as a weaving shed, the Sandygate Mill had a floor area of 2,170 yards, with warehouse storage on two floors of 2,000 yards floor space. Water to supply the one Lancashire boiler was obtained from the near by Leeds and Liverpool Canal, this was 'new' in 1913. Steam from the boiler ran a 250hp beam engine.

SANDYGATE SHED, SANDYGATE, BURNLEY

The Sandygate Shed was the mill above Neptune Street on Sandygate, not to be confused with Sandygate Mill, higher up behind the former Waterloo Hotel. George Slater built the Sandygate Shed around 1880, as part of his 'empire', and at one time we know that it had a six-storey warehouse built across from the warehouse at the end of Slater Terrace. Sandygate Shed was demolished in quite recent years.

SCAR TOP MILL, SCAR TOP, OFF CHURCH STREET, BURNLEY

Scar Top Mill is now demolished. The mill dated from around the early 1840s, and was worked Law and Veevers in 1843 and in 1848 by Jonathan Law, and it had two sheds with 10,300 spindles. R. and H. Law, cotton spinners and manufacturers, were working the mill in 1868 when it had become a weaving factory, with a beam engine of 50hp, and had 350 looms. Two boilers provided the power for the engine. It was worked by J.R. Cooper and Co. (Burnley) Ltd in 1923, who by 1934 had 621 looms 'stopped' due to a depression in trade. The mill at this time it was stated was being taken over by a 'firm of botanical brewers'. I think this might have been Joseph Whewell's 'pop works'.

SLATER'S MILL

(See Clock Tower Mill)

SMITHFIELD MILL

This mill was worked from around 1840 through to the 1890s and is another name for the Industry Mill, Stanley Street (see also that entry).

SPA MILL, SPA STREET, OFF JUNCTION STREET, BURNLEY

The Spa Mill was owned by J.W. Whittam in the 1930s. It consisted of a basement warehouse, containing 680 yards of floor space; a weaving shed, containing 2,330 yards of floor space, and a store with 170 yards of floor space. The buildings were constructed of stone with slate roof and the usual northern lights to the weaving shed, with a total site area of 3,380 yards. The mill

A view of Spa Mill taken from the canal.

adjoined the Leeds and Liverpool Canal, from which the water for the boiler was obtained. There was a Lancashire boiler fitted with a Green's economiser, and Proctor's stoker. The boiler fed the 1,250hp tandem compound steam engine. The Spa Mill was being worked by John A. Cowpe Ltd in 1923, and under the same name, the mill's 738 looms were 'stopped and unoccupied' in 1924. The Spa Motor Co. occupied the mill site in the mid-1940s. The building has now been demolished, following a disastrous fire, and all that remains are part of the perimeter walls. New housing now occupies the site. In its latter years the mill was occupied by Sutcliffe and Clarkson Ltd which was founded in 1911 and which manufactured electric blankets and cotton cloth. One might wonder where the spa was actually from which the mill took its name. The Spa Mill dated from 1878, and was the place of a fatal accident in 1916: in November that year, James Henry Sandy of Cotton Street, Whittelfield was caught in the shafting and killed. He and his wife ran ten looms between them, and while his wife had gone an errand, James tried to put back some belting on a loom next to theirs – in doing so he lost his life.

SPA FIELD MILL (OR SPAFIELD MILL), CORNER OF PARLIAMENT STREET, AND TODMORDEN ROAD, BURNLEY

This mill dates from the 1860s. John Kay was working it in 1865, and appeared to do so for most of its life, along with the Burnley Wood Mills. John Kay was born in Darwen about 1817: by the early 1880s John was living at No. 60 Todmorden Road where he described himself as a 'Cotton Spinner and manufacturer employing 630 people'. On Wednesday, 15 May 1878, a crowd of many thousands went to Mr Kay's premises on Parliament Street, and threw stones at the windows. The police charged several times, and the mayor read the Riot Act. Eventually, soldiers were summoned, but by the time they arrived the rioters had ignited the warehouse. The building was almost gutted, and not until a military chain was thrown around the mill could the fire brigade even begin to tackle the blaze. Even then stones were thrown over the heads of the guards, and hosepipes cut. Later the strikers went up to Towneley Villas where Mr Kay lived and once again windows were broken and stones thrown. The following day a crowd of around 300 gathered at Kay's Mill, but heavy rain drove them away. As night drew in, the crowd gathered at the centre of town near Manchester Road, and again the Riot Act was read from the window of the Thorn Hotel. Troops were called in and they cleared the streets, and although an attempt was made to attack the Whittlefield Mill little damage was done and the crowds dispersed. Over the next weeks the strikers returned to work and by the middle of June all had accepted the 10 per cent reduction in wages. Twenty-four weavers, mostly youths, were charged at the Assizes. Three of those were sent to prison for five years, and seven for six months: the rest got four months or less. The strike though proved a victory for the manufacturers, and by the end of 1879, the weavers' wages had been reduced down to 20 or 25 per cent of the original price. Once again soup kitchens were brought into use to feed the hungry weavers and their families.

The Spafield mill had over 1,000 looms in 1934, but only half of them were running due to a depression in trade. There was a serious fire at the Spa Field Mill in November 1938, when the 'newly formed members of the A.R.P. auxiliary fire service helped the regular fire brigade to put out the fire'. This may have spelt the end for Spafield Mill. On 8 February 1939 by instruction of Messrs John Kay and Sons Ltd there was a sale by auction of much of the mill plant and machinery, including the steam-power plant, grey warp on weavers' beams and cloth and weft.

Just before the fire, in May 1938, one of Mr Kay's most loyal employees, James Metcalfe, took retirement after sixty-two years with the firm. He remembered well the troubled times of 1878 when the crowds attacked the mill. James was the son of John and Mary Metcalfe who used to live on Tarleton Street – he began work at the mill in 1876 aged just twelve years old. At the age of eighteen he became a book-keeper and cloth-looker at the mill, a position which he kept until he retired. His retirement gifts included a purse of money from the weavers, and a cardigan jacket and some tobacco from his workmates in the warehouse. James Hargreaves, plumber's merchant, now occupies the site and all that remains are a few perimeter walls incorporated into the plumbers' merchants. The name of the mill comes from a former spa near here 'discovered' by one of the Towneley family, a spring of pure water thought to have medicinal properties.

SPRING GARDENS MILL, TURF STREET, BURNLEY

The Spring Garden Mill is mentioned in 1848, when worked by the Pickering Brothers: it was also known as 'Pickering's spinning mill' but probably dates from around 1843. Certainly it shows up on the OS Map for the year 1851. James and Bernard Cowban were listed as cotton spinners and manufacturers at Turf Street in 1868, although it was being worked by Fulton and Slater in 1879. Skipton-born William K. Fulton lived at Willow Bank on Brooklands Road off Todmorden Road and he stated that at this time that he employed 159 adults and thirty-six children. Many will remember this former mill as being 'Taskers' and is now the RDA Trading Store (2001). The present-day car park at the rear of the mill was formerly the weaving shed here. The mill was used for cotton-goods manufacture, and was worked by W.E. Browning Ltd, cotton manufacturers, in 1923. Shortly after this date there was a depression in the trade and Browning's had over 500 looms stopped. It was around this time that parts of the mill were let out to others. These included a firm of cabinet makers, and a firm of scouring stone manufacturers. The building consisted of a four-storey mill and a one-storey shed, all stone-built. There is nothing architecturally enlightening or beautiful about Spring Garden Mill, it was simply built to serve a purpose – that of cotton spinning and manufacturing.

SPRINGFIELD MILL, WATERLOO ROAD, BURNLEY

The mill was worked by Lancaster Brothers in the 1920s. However, in August 1928 they were selling by auction various machines and plant belonging got the Springfield Mill. These included 1,227 power looms, a patent knotting machine, tape sizing machines, winding and beaming frames, looming and twisting frames, plaiting machines, bobbins and skips. The mill formerly worked 1, 227 looms, but following a drop in demand and a deep depression of trade the mill was reported in 1934 as 'being in the course of demolition'. The mill dated from 1878. Arthur Lancaster, of Lancaster Brothers, lived at 'Storrs' No. 169 Manchester Road, Burnley and William Lancaster JP lived at 'Morningside' on Carlton Road.

SPRINGHILL SHED, SPRINGHILL ROAD, BURNLEY

The Springhill Shed was opened in March 1882, as a weaving shed, when the mill engine was also started, being built by Berry and Smith. In the mid-1930s the Springhill Shed was owned by The Rosehill Mill Co. Ltd. The weaving shed itself contained 4,800 yards of floor space, with warehouse accommodation at basement level, ground floor and first floor of 2,760 yards floor space. The building is of brickwork construction with slate roof. Water for the two Lancashire boilers was obtained from a private reservoir, and supplied steam to a 600hp horizontal cross compound engine with a sixteen-rope drive flywheel. This reservoir gave its name to Reservoir Street to the rear of the mill. The mill was worked by the Clevelands Manufacturing Co. Ltd in 1923. Under this firm the mill had 496 looms, but in 1934 they were all stopped. 'The whole of this mill is now closed', said a report at this time. Garments Distributors Ltd occupied the premises in the mid-1940s, and today (2007) parts of the former cotton shed are occupied by Burnley College. Many however will remember Springhill Shed as being the 'knicker factory' worked by Elgin Manufacturing Co., which was a member of the famed Courtaulds Group.

SPRUCE MILL, SPRUCE STREET, OFF FINSLEYGATE

Spruce Mill, now demolished was located beside the Leeds and Liverpool Canal near the top of Finsleygate, on the left-hand side before the canal bridge, coming from Manchester Road. Spruce Mill, dated at least from the 1852. In the time of the Cotton Famine (1862–64), the owner failed, and had to fall back on keeping a small draper's shop in Manchester. David Read Ltd was working at the Spruce Mill in 1910, and used the premises as a cotton-waste shop. The mill was worked by Button and Guthrie Ltd in 1923, who were also listed as being the owners in 1935. The mill used to have 461 looms. The weaving shed contained about 5,000

Springhill Shed.

yards of floor space, and had a good water supply, presumably from the canal. However, at the latter date, the mill was said to be 'in a bad state of repair', and, 'the mill had been standing empty for some considerable time and is badly damaged'. The mill was worked by William Hargreaves in the mid-1860s.

STANLEY MILL, SHACKLETON STREET, BURNLEY

The chimney at the Stanley Mill was 'christened' in 1867. Stanley Mill appears to have been extended over the years and is a typical 'dark satanic mill'. It bears a date stone '1891' and was built by Robert Emmott and his family. Notice too the lintel that bears the name 'Stanley Mill'. The mill was worked by Robert Emmott Ltd in 1923 and 1945, and still survives near Duke Bar. The imposing blackened stone frontage held the warehouses and boiler and engine rooms, and at the back is a large weaving shed.

The story of Robert Emmott is quite a remarkable one: Robert was born in June 1820 at Haggate of poor parents. He was also disadvantaged in his early years by having no education whatsoever. It was only when he attained manhood that he was able to attend evening classes run by John Sutcliffe, a manufacturer, that Robert was able to get a smattering of the three R's. In his very early years Robert worked as a handloom weaver and progressed to do the looming and warping for other weavers. As the old handlooms died out Robert followed his employment at Harle Syke as a loomer and twister – he was also a man of very careful habits and was able to save a little each week. At last, in 1854, he took on an important part in the forming of a company at Harle Syke whose purpose was to erect a small cotton shed, the

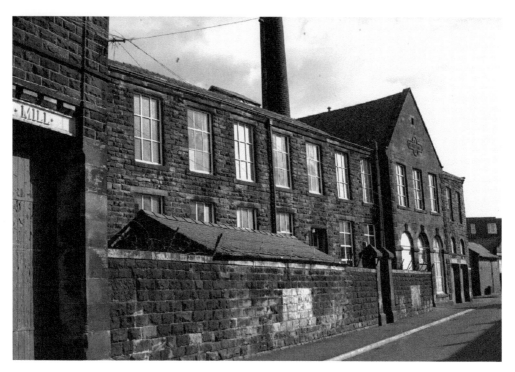

Stanley Mill.

first weaving shed at Harle Syke. This was later known as the 'Old Shed' and was built on the self-help principal and was capable of containing around 800 looms. The American War of 1864–65 had a drastic effect on the cotton industry as a whole, not only in East Lancashire, but throughout the country. At the close of the conflict the company was reformed with the building being left in the hands of the old company and the looms were sold off to the shareholders. Robert Emmott's share of the looms numbered twenty-four. Then, along with other workmen Robert formed a company with about 120 looms worked under the title of Robert Emmott and Co.

In 1871 Robert moved to Burnley and went into partnership with three of his brothers-in-law; Henry, William and Thomas Burrows, who traded as Burrow Brothers and Co. They started in business at Albert Shed on Canning Street running 157 looms, and two years later were able to move to Caldervale Shed with 300 looms. In 1875 the firm was able to purchase of Mr Smallpage about 500 looms at Gannow Shed. They then ran the business from both mills. In 1878 the partnership between the Burrow's and Robert Emmott was dissolved. However, Robert stayed on at Caldervale Shed. By 1887 Robert was able to take over the Bishop House Mill at Burnley Lane, where he increased the number of his looms to 1,250. In 1890, Robert decided to retire and made a gift of his cotton business to his close family members, Hartley Emmott, Thomas Emmott, Mrs Atkinson, Mrs Briggs and Mrs Stephenson. The following year they built the extensive Stanley Mill on Shackleton Street. The firm was still known as Robert Emmott, and from Stanley Mills ran 1,830 looms. Robert passed away in February 1897 and was returned to his native village and was buried at the Haggate Chapel there. The firm of George Ratcliffe and Sons (Felts) Ltd had been manufacturing felts here at Stanley Mill for over forty years, but in 2002 it was announced that the firm would close with a loss of fifty jobs.

STONEYHOLME SHED, GROSVENOR STREET, BURNLEY

The Stoneyholme Shed dated from 1865, and in 1868, was being worked by the trustees of Wilkinson Altham, who had sixty-seven looms in operation. In 1879 the mill was worked by Edward Houlding junior. Edward lived at No. 167 Manchester Road, Burnley and employed 321 hands at this time. The mill was worked by Maxfield and Co. Ltd in 1923, who also operated the Springhill Sheds. Also operating here in 1923 was the firm of John Henry Preston, cotton manufacturers, and John Proctor and Sons Ltd. By the year 1935, the Stoneyholme Shed was owned by J. Pickard, metal merchant, of Ashfield Road. The original mill consisted of two weaving sheds, one containing 6,630 yards of floor space, the other 730 yards of floor space. In addition there was a two-storey warehouse that contained 3,200 yards of floor space. The Stoneyholme Shed at the latter date contained hoists, beams runways, steam heating, gas lighting, sprinklers, fire-proof doors, and was complete with looms and shafting, with 800 looms in store. The mill was available to let at an annual rent of £1,000, excluding power, or to sell at £10,000 excluding machinery. Water was obtained from the River Calder, which adjoined the site, and fed the two Lancashire boilers, which were new in 1919. The boilers, were fitted with Proctor's Stokers, and Green's economisers, and fed steam to a 600hp cross compound engine, that had a sixteen-rope drive flywheel. The site of Stoneyholme Shed was taken by the site of Council offices and the waste disposal site off Princess Way. Little remains of the former mill other than boundary walls and the Holme Road side.

SYDNEY STREET MILL

Few details are known of this mill, which is mentioned in a directory for the year 1879, when it was worked by Ogle and Pickard. Andrew Ogle was born at Bolton le Moor Lancashire around 1829 and he employed in the early 1880s as a 'master cotton spinner' 121 adult males, 176 adult females and twenty-eight children. He lived at No. 39 Westgate, the large house just before Clifton Street, now part of East Lancashire Health Drug Clinic. Sydney Street, from which the mill took its name, was on the lower end of Bankhouse Street on the viaduct side and the mill appears to have later become the Victoria brass works and, later still, Turner and Smith's joinery works.

THORNEYBANK MILL, TRAFALGAR STREET, BURNLEY

The Thorneybank Mill still stands: it is the first shed on the right-hand side coming from Manchester Road, beyond the former Nelson pub. The mill was constructed around 1860 for Graham and Shepherd, as a cotton spinning and weaving shed. In the mid-1880s, the mill stopped cotton spinning and moved over to cotton weaving entirely, and at this time was being run by Walter Shepherd. Walter lived at Carlton Road, just up Manchester Road. The mill was worked by Thomas Catlow Ltd in 1923, who is also listed as being the owner of the mill in 1935.

Throstle Mill, also known as Elm Street Shed.

The mill consisted of three separate weaving sheds, the No. 1 had 1,000 yards of floor space, No.2 1920 yards of floor space, and the No. 3 920 yards of floor space. In addition the warehouse contained on three floors 2,300 yards of floor space. In 1934, the Thorneybank Mill of Thomas Catlow Ltd had 947 looms, but was 'stopped and unoccupied'. The mill was to be sold in 1935, by which time, all the looms and shafting had removed, along with the power plant. The mill is stone construction with slate roof and the usual northern lights to the weaving sheds. A plan to demolish the mill in 2004 and to build twenty-five apartments was refused.

THROSTLE MILL, DANESHOUSE ROAD, ELM STREET JUNCTION, BURNLEY

Throstle Mill was worked by the Thornber family, and still survives. It dates from around 1863. (Also known as Elm Street Shed: see that entry).

TOP FACTORY, BROWN STREET, BURNLEY

This was the name given to one of William Hopwood's early factories built in 1820 in Brown Street, a little beyond Veever Street. It was probably on the corner of what was called 'Mill Street' on Fishwick's Map of 1827. John Brennand also worked a mill named Brown Street Mill in 1865, according to a directory for that year. Nothing remains: the area has since been redeveloped.

TOPPER'S MILL, WESTGATE, BURNLEY

According to Walter Bennett in his *History of Burnley*, Topper's Mill was built in 1830, 'beyond the Westgate Chapel', and destroyed in a fire. John Lowe, however, in *Burnley* puts this mill on St James' Street, near Cow Lane, on the Cross Keys side, and says that the mill, a woollen mill, was built prior to 1787. Wherever it was, there are no remains now.

TRAFALGAR MILL, TRAFALGAR STREET, BURNLEY

The mill, built in 1846 as a mule-spinning mill, was worked by Thompson & Moore in 1848. William Thompson worked Trafalgar Mill in 1868, and it continued to be connected with the Thompson family, with this and the Trafalgar Shed being worked by W. & T. Thompson, in 1945. The section nearest the Leeds and Liverpool Canal were built in 1867, as a boiler-house for the mill. Later, in 1872, the section of mill nearest Trafalgar Street was completed. The small single storey building near the footbridge, with 'Trafalgar Mill' over the doorway, was an office at the same time. The tower was also built at this time, with an extension in 1888 built to carry the tank for water in case of fire, and for topping up the engine boilers. A fine example of 'northern lights' can be seen from the footbridge. These were used to provide maximum light into the mills, while at the same time avoiding direct sunlight, which would dry out the cotton threads. This part of the building was built around 1867, the same time as the canalside extension. The Thompson family were great benefactors to the town: James Witham Thompson gave money for Thompson Park that opened in 1930, and William Thompson gave money for the William Thompson Recreation Centre, which was only recently demolished, its place being taken by the new St Peter's Centre.

TRAFALGAR SHED, TRAFALGAR STREET, BURNLEY

The site of the Trafalgar Shed has now been taken over by Kitchen's Garage, but which dated from around 1860. Partial remains of the former mill can be seen as a retaining wall at the back near the canal. The mill at one time contained 1,227 power looms and had a total floor area of over 7,800 square yards. Two Lancashire boilers, each 30ft by 7ft 6in, powered a 600 hp horizontal cross compound steam engine, which was made by the Burnley Iron Works. The Trafalgar Shed was one of W. & T. Thompson's Mills who also worked the Premier Mill at Great Harwood – the firm had 1,250 looms at work in the 1940s at the Trafalgar Shed.

TUNNEL STREET SHED, TUNNEL STREET, BURNLEY

Tunnel Street Shed dated from around 1890, and was worked by Simpson and Baldwin, in 1934, who had 845 looms – but all were stopped due to a slump in trade. The mill was a typical weaving shed with northern light roof. The firm did apparently recover; they were running the mill in 1945. Although I don't remember the mill being pulled down, I can remember its ruins from around the mid-1960s, it became what we knew as the 'old fac' – a childhood pleasure land. Interestingly, the shed was actually below ground at the Tunnel Street end by as much as 20ft. There are no remains of Tunnel Street Shed – housing now occupies the site.

A view of Trafalgar Shed, taken from near the footbridge.

The weavers at work in Trafalgar Shed.

VEEVERS MILL, VEEVERS STREET, BURNLEY

This is what was probably called 'The Bottom Factory', built in about 1790, according to James Howell, and was near the site of the paint shop, formerly the Salvation Army Hostel, on Calder Street. It was built by Sagar Veevers, hence the naming of the street. Nothing remains; it closed around 1830. Sagar Veevers was listed under 'gentry' in a directory for 1792, along with people such as the Towneley's, Ormerod's, Hammerton's and Halsted's. 'The spinning factory in Veevers Street, was three storeys high, 20 yards long and ten yards broad, which also had a steam engine of 5 hp., adjoining the mill, was a warehouse and spinning shed', says Walter Bennett in *History of Burnley*, Vol. III page 179.

VICTORIA MILL, TRAFALGAR STREET, BURNLEY

Victoria Mill was originally started by the Massey's, (they of brewing fame and Masseys' Brewery), as a spinning mill. Massey and Co. are listed as being cotton manufacturers in 1824, at Win Hall (sic), Whin Hill, Sandygate. The Victoria Mill was built in 1854, for Edward Stocks Massey, as a throstle-spinning mill. Throstle spinning was a method of spinning using a powered version of Arkwright's water frame. John Massey is listed in 1868, at Victoria Mill, Trafalgar Street, and lived at Hawk House, Reedley. Edward Stocks Massey was running the mill by 1887, and it contained between 18,000 and 20,000 spindles. On the ground floor there were sixteen double carding engines, five pairs of roving engines and two roving frames. On 31 January 1856 it was reported that:

> About twelve o'clock on Tuesday night, a gentleman, returning home from a visit in the outskirts of the town discovered a fire in the room above the engine-house of the mill recently erected by Mr. J. Massey, on the higher side of the canal, near the Mitre Inn. The alarm being quickly given, a fire engine and the town's hose proceeded quickly to the spot...

There was another great fire here in March 1882 that caused damage to the mill amounting to over £20,000. Soon after this date, however, Massey's, along with eight other spinning firms locally, ceased to trade as spinning mills due to competition from the Oldham ring-spinning machines. This was one of the main reasons for the final and general diminution of Burnley's spinning industry – the competition from Oldham, where spinners, about 1880, adopted ring-spinning machines, each with 80,000–100,000 spindles. The new invention enabled cotton to be spun at 1d a pound cheaper than on the throstle and mule machines, so that Burnley manufacturers found it more profitable to buy yarn from Oldham than manufacture it for use in their own sheds.

The mill remained empty until around 1890, when the Victoria Mill Co. bought it for use as both spinning and weaving, but just over ten years later it was dealing in cotton-waste. The Victoria Mill still survives, albeit in a dilapidated condition: it is the first mill on the left coming from the Mitre Junction going towards Manchester Road. The owner of the Victoria Mill in 1935 was R. J. Patchett, of the 'Woodlands' Queensbury, near Bradford. It was stated that there was no permanent power plant on the premises at this time, and that a number of parts had been let off to various tenants. A total of 2,420 yards of floor space was available to sell or let. Hammond and Co., mattress maker occupied the mill in the mid-1940s. Later tenants might include those listed on the notice board, which is still visible: these include 'Leyfield Products',

Victoria Mill, Trafalgar.

'Victoria Tannery' and 'Boldsworth Holdings'. The main structure at Victoria Mill is four-storeys high, with a six-storey tower attached, built as extensions to the mill in 1889 on the site of the original mill. The buildings to the rear of the main one are alterations and additions, much of which was partially demolished both in the 1930s and 1970s.

WALKER HEY MILL, GEORGE STREET, BURNLEY

Walker Hey Mill was rebuilt in 1920. This mill occupied in part the site later taken by the Meadows Mill, on George Street, it is the mill on the left-hand side of the footbridge at the George Street end going over to Trafalgar Street, now the Besglos Works. The 'Walkerhey Mill' (as it was sometimes spelt) dated from at least the 1840s, being worked by Roberts and Walton in 1843. In later years it was worked by James and William Roberts (1868) and Edward Houlding junior, in 1887, who also worked at the Trafalgar Mill. The mill was four-storeys high and 'twenty windows long' and adjacent to the Leeds and Liverpool Canal. The ground floor contained 220 looms, the second floor was occupied with carding machinery, the third was used for throstle spinning, and the top floor for mule spindles. In all there were 8,000 throstle spindles, and 445 looms, half of which were in an adjoining shed but run by the same steam engine. The mill employed around 200 operatives. The mill was gutted in a fire in May 1887, when 'a large portion of the roof fell with a crash, as did a quantity of the spinning machinery in the top room'. The Walker Hey Mill is marked on the map of 1851.

Walshaw Mill.

WALSHAW MILL, TALBOT STREET, HARLE SYKE

Walshaw Mill was a stone-built cotton-weaving shed built in 1905, with a large slender red-brick chimney which used to have, until quite recently, a slight 'bend' in it. The mill, when started, had 586 narrow Burnley looms, but at its peak had 1,100 looms in operation weaving cloth for export, and was worked in the main by the Walshaw Mill Co. Ltd which survived up until the early 1970s. Following its closure the mill became the headquarters of the Hills Pharmaceutical Ltd. The mill was built on the site of a small stone quarry. The engine house here has a fine arched stone window. Much of this information is taken from Roger Frost's *A Lancashire Township*. In 1940 the Walshaw Mill Co. Ltd were running 1,092 looms; Thomas Constantine was the mill manager at this time and lived at 2 Wynotham Street down near the General Hospital. Thomas began his career with the Walshaw Mill Co. when he was aged just sixteen in around 1897. He went on to become the inside manager director and the firm's representative at Manchester. Thomas died in September 1952 and was buried at Haggate.

WATER STREET MILL, WATER STREET, BURNLEY

Water Street was an old street in the 'Wapping' district of Burnley, off Bridge Street. The Water Street Mill was being worked by William Tickle and Nephew at Nos 32 Water Street, and Bridge Street in 1818 through to 1824, and perhaps a little beyond. William Tickle and Nephew were listed under 'cotton manufacturers and spinners'. There were a number of other cotton spinners and manufacturers on Bridge Street at this time, including Henry Crooke senior, and William Dale.

The Water Street Mill survived for just ten years until around 1830. There are no remains; this area of town has long since been developed for other uses.

WATERLOO SHED, TRAFALGAR STREET, BURNLEY

Waterloo Shed was operated in 1879 by John F. Coulthurst, cotton manufacturer with 444 looms. John Forest Coulthurst lived on Albion Street with his wife Hannah and daughter Elizabeth Alice, and he employed thirty-two males and females and five children at his Waterloo Shed around this time. This is the shed on the far right-hand side of the Trafalgar Mill, as you face the footbridge going over to the 'Meadows' district. The mill is now known as Celtique Mill, and was built in the 1860s as a cotton-weaving shed. In the 1930s during a time of a great depression in the cotton industry, the mill was worked by the Waterloo Manufacturing Co., who unfortunately had all 417 looms 'stopped' due to lack of trade.

WATERSIDE MILL, ROSEGROVE, BURNLEY

Worked by Mitchell Brothers (Burnley) Ltd, cotton manufacturers in 1923, and capable of running 1,073 looms. It was taken over by 1934 by the firm of Burnley Components Ltd, an electrical, mechanical and textile engineers. Waterside Mill is the name given to, but rarely used, for the mill besides Maden Fold Bridge, and before Lowerhouse Lane. The mill commenced weaving about 1915, before the impending depression in the cotton trade. The name 'Waterside Mill' can been seen at the bottom of Langham Street, and the date '1914'. Charles Henry Mitchell, one of the partners, lived at St Annes-on-Sea. The Waterside Mill later became 'Burco' electric washers', later still Burco-Dean. The mill still survives, predominately a red-bricked weaving-shed type of structure, but has been put to other uses.

WESTGATE SHED, SANDYGATE, BURNLEY

These buildings date from 1886, being built as a cotton-weaving mill, when it was worked by Butterworth and Dickinson Ltd with 400 looms. By 1933 a deep depression in the cotton trade meant these 400 looms were stopped. This is the mill directly behind the Plane Tree Inn. It was built in the traditional manner, with warehouse accommodation to one side and weaving sheds, with northern light roofing to the other side. Just above the Plane Tree can be seen substantial steelwork shoring up this part of the mill. In 2004 permission was given to convert part of the mill into a children's party venue and workshops which survives at the time of writing.

WHIN HILL MILL, ANDYGATE, BURNLEY

Whin Hill, or Win Hill, is the old name for the bottom part of Sandygate. The Whin Hill Mill was directly across from the present-day 'Old Malthouse' on Sandygate. Massey and Co. are listed as being cotton manufacturers in 1824 at Win Hall (sic). The mill was built in 1820 as a worsted and woollen mill. The mill was named 'Massey's' on the map of 1851. There are no remains of this mill – it is long gone. The *Burnley Advertiser* of 16 January 1858, contained the following report:

Waterside Mill.

On Friday evening, the 8th. Inst., the workpeople in the employ of John Massey were regaled with tea in the new room adjoining the mill in Sandy Gate Meadow. The room which was decorated with evergreens, is, we understand, being developed solely for the use of the operatives for mental improvement, after the hours of labour. On this occasion, the third annual treat, the tea was served out by friends of their worthy employer, and full justice was done to the excellent fare provided, after which the cloth was drawn and a most interesting meeting commenced. This was addressed by Mr. Massey, the Rev. Stroyan, Mr. Smyth, and several of the workpeople. Mr. Massey being called to the chair. The meeting broke up a little after ten o'clock. The workpeople being well satisfied with the pleasing entertainment that had been afforded to them.

WHITTLEFIELD MILL, JUNCTION STREET, BURNLEY

This mill was next door to the Olive Mount Mill on Junction Street, furthest away from Padiham Road, and was worked in 1868 by Stephenson and Collinge, cotton spinners and manufacturers. Later it was worked by Robert Pickles Ltd. The buildings are now demolished, and there are no remains. The Whittlefield Mill, a spinning mill, bore the date '1861' and was the scene of a serious fire in December 1914. The fire was so fierce that one of the walls on the canal side fell into the water, with some of the masonry falling on to the opposite banking and the heat setting fire to a telegraph pole some distance away. The four-storey preparation plant was completely burnt out, although the weaving shed, engine house and chimney were undamaged. Very little of the part of the mill where the fire originated was left standing without fear of it falling down. It was decided therefore the following day to pull down all the outer walls on safety grounds. The mill was offered for sale on 17 June 1891 at the Bull Hotel on Manchester Road, and described as follows:

All that modern weaving shed called 'Whittlefield Mill' Burnley holding 1,2,36 looms comprising of brick and stone buildings (part fireproof) two double flued steam boilers 30 foot by 7 foot 6 inches fitted with Proctor's patent stokers. 120 pipes, pair of high and low pressure beam steam engines, one horizontal steam engine for driving taping machines, mill gearing, shafting, steam gas and water pipes and other attached fixtures therein. The mill is on the banks of the Leeds and Liverpool Canal from which it draws water. The land forming the site is subject to a yearly ground rent of about £54. This lot will be subject to a lease to Messrs J. F. Bleakley and Brothers for supplying to them room and power for 744 looms and 2 tape machines, making a total of £1563 12s 0p, per annum...

WHITTLEFIELD SHED, JUNCTION STREET, BURNLEY

Whittlefield Shed was worked by William Burrows and Sons Ltd in 1923. All the building still survives, but is now derelict and probably soon faces demolition. At the time of writing a fine stone-built circular chimney survives on the canalside. In 1888 room and power in Whittlefield Shed was leased for 38s a loom, to which was added an extra £70 a year as rent for space for taping machines, etc. In November 1887, the 'Whittlefield Self-Help Co.' was formed to take over 542 looms from J.H. Whitaker in Whittlefield shed. In the year 1907, the Whittlefield Sheds were being worked by Messrs Burrows. In March that year, thirteen-year-old Harriet Dunham of Tunnel Street was clearing some waste from under the looms. Her hair caught in the shafting, and she was literally scalped. Happily she survived, but it shows how dangerous mills can be, especially for the young and inexperienced, and the horrendous tasks they had to perform. There was another harrowing experience for the workpeople at Whittlefield Shed in 1911: when they returned from lunch in March that year, the mill engine was stopped for no apparent reason. On investigation they found the engine tenter Thomas Henry Haworth hanging from a rope dead in the waste cellar. Later a verdict of 'suicide while temporarily insane' was recorded on Haworth, who was aged just thirty-seven years.

WILKINSON'S MILL, SAUNDER BANK, BURNLEY

This was one of the earliest mills in the Saunder Bank area of Burnley and dated from around the late 1790s. The mill was built by Jeremy Wilkinson and continued by his son. It later became part of the Butterworth and Dickinson's iron foundry. Near here in 1824 was also a cotton factory belonging to Edward Gregson. There are no remains of Wilkinson's Mill: it is long gone.

WISEMAN STREET MILL

Wiseman Street Mill was the alternative name for Oak Mount Mill (see also that entry). The mill engine here has been preserved and is occasionally opened to the public, as part of the Weavers'

Wood Top Mill.

Triangle Visitors Centre. In the 1940s this mill was operating 834 looms and worked by Sutcliffe and Clarkson.

WOOD TOP MILL, VILLIERS STREET, BURNLEY

Thomas Emmott and Sons worked Wood Top Mill in 1923. By 1935, the sheds were owned by the Wood Top Room and Power Co. and had a total floor space of 12,630 yards. Under the Room and Power Co. in 1934, there were the firms of Rinard Manufacturing Co., who ran 550 looms; the Bartle Hill Manufacturing Co., which was 'stopped' due to a slump in trade; the Gordale manufacturing Co. Ltd, who were here in 1940 and who operated 194 looms. Harold Hargreaves was the manager of this firm. Two reservoirs belonging to, and adjacent to, the mill supplied the water for two Lancashire boilers. These supplied the steam to an 800hp horizontal cross compound steam engine with gear drive.

The Lucas Organisation took over the Wood Top Mill in 1941, for the design, development, testing and manufacture of aircraft gas-turbine engines. This was begun with the W.2.B; the first British Jet engine aircraft. In the early days, this development took place in strict security: the Lucas employees at Hargher Clough Mill knew nothing of what their colleges at Wood Top were up to, even those the mills were only 300 yards apart! These precautions were carried on until 1944, when the existence of a jet-propelled aircraft was announced to the world. To mark this occasion a squadron of Meteor jet aircraft performed aerobatics over Burnley for the benefit of the Lucas employees. The Wood top works were further enlarged in 1942, and the test facilities were among the finest in the country, providing unlimited scope for research, development and testing. *Worker's Playtime* was broadcast from here in 1956. The mill survived until recent years, when it was run by A.I.T.

WOODBINE MILL, WOODBINE ROAD, BURNLEY

This mill was built in 1906. It was worked by Thomas Walton and Son both in 1923 and 1945, who operated 1,063 looms at the latter date, manufacturing printers, bleachers, haircords, and poplins. It later became Thomas Ashworth's Ltd, die-casters, and was demolished only recently; the site is now taken by modern housing. Part of Woodbine Mill was used for a number of years by Northern Textiles, but in April 2003 the shock announcement came that the firm was to close down with a loss of 11,120 jobs. The mill takes its name from the former Woodbine Cottage and Farm, which later still gave its name to the Woodbine Housing Estate. This mill was a fine, predominately red-brick weaving shed, with some fine stonework incorporated in the design of the building.

WOODFIELD MILL, TRAFALGAR STREET, BURNLEY

Woodfield Mill is the first mill on the right coming from the Mitre Junction on Trafalgar Street, going towards the Manchester Road end. The mill began work in 1889, although the tank above bears the date 1888. Notice the fine casting over the door on Trafalgar Street that bears the mill name. The mill was built as a weaving shed, and contained 5,829 yards of floor space in the weaving shed and 2,771 yards of floor space used as warehouse accommodation. The building is brick built and occupies 6,697 square yards. Canal water was used to power the two Lancashire boilers that supplied the cross compound steam engine. In 1934, the Woodfield mill was worked by Hooper, Wright and Spencer Ltd who had 470 looms 'stopped'. The mill itself was unoccupied at this time. The Woodfield Mill was operated for many years by Robert Tunstill. In 1922, the mill was purchased by Thomas Tunstill, a nephew of Robert for £37,000, and continued to be run under the title of 'Thomas Tunstill' for many years. By 1948, the firm of Lupton and Place were occupying the Woodfield Mill. The former cotton mill still survives to this day, although used for other purposes.

YATEFIELD MILL, COG LANE, BURNLEY

The Yatefield Mill was the large spinning mill. It was begun by the Haslam's in 1863, at the bottom end of Cog Lane, near its junction with Gannow Lane. Halsam Street that used to run down in front of the St Mary Magdalene's church recalled the family. It was built by James Duckett (of the later sanitary-pipe manufacturing firm), who had premises on Blannel Street. James was originally a builder, but following complaints by the Haslam's over the quality of his work (unfounded by all accounts), he swore he would never built again once he had finished the Yatefield Mill. He then entered into making bricks, and later still sanitary ware – he never looked back.

The mill later became, as many will remember, the Brook Bond Factory. Being brought up in this area, the author remembers watching the Brook Bond tea packets go past as he stared through the windows of the former mill on the Cog Lane side. My mother also used to work at the chocolate factory at the rear of the mill – consequently he had many friends and vast amounts of chocolate.

The Yatefield Mill was put up for sale by the Haslam's in 1928, who then moved on to Colne. This was time of deep depression in the cotton trade. Haslam's were stated to have over 1,000 looms 'stopped' at Yatefield Mill. The mill was advertised again in 1937, when it contained 26,460 weft mules, 21,088 ring twist spindles and 1,058 twill and plain looms. Included was the power plant, which consisted of a horizontal tandem compound engine, beam engines, fire pumps, and three cage hoists. Nothing remains of Yatefield Mill, which was swept aside during the construction of the M65 motorway.

Although the Haslam Brothers moved out of Yatefield Mill in 1928, it was still in their ownership in 1935. The total weaving space on two floors was 16,530 yards. In the spinning section there was 10,950 yards of floor space on five floors. Water for the steam engines was obtained from the Leeds and Liverpool Canal, although in 1935 all the power plant and machinery had been removed. In 1934, it was reported that Yatefield Mill was being run by T. Tunstill Ltd, but all the 955 looms were stopped. There was a report in the local newspaper in 1938 that the Yatefield Mill could be adapted for use in the manufacture of shoes and slippers, (see below). This may have come to fruition or indeed may not have: certainly Brooke Bond and Co. Ltd, tea directors were at Yatefield Mill by the mid-1940s, and they pulled out in January 1970. This fine multi-storey mill was demolished to make way for the M65 Motorway, its other claim to fame is that, as far as I'm aware, this was the first building to be sandblasted in Burnley in the early 1960s. *Burnley Advertiser*, 15 January 1870:

To be sold by auction by Mr Matthew Watson on Monday 24 January 1870 in that part of Yatefield Mill, situated at Gannow near Burnley, lately occupied by Mr James Arnold the following valuable machinery and other effects.

180 POWER LOOMS of 43 inch reed space, by Thomas Sagar with temples beams and weights, complete, all in really first class working condition; Double geared cloth press by Sagar. 1, plaiting machine, a large quantity of strapping, healds, reeds, shuttles, weft cans, change wheels, spare beams, weight, loom chains etc. Also, tacklers bench, vice cupboard and tools; cloth tables, clock, loom rods, twisting and looming frames, cloth racks, and many other sundry articles. Sale to commence at eleven o'clock in the forenoon.

Catalogues may be had at the office of the Auctioneer, 53 Manchester Road, Burnley on and after the 17th instant. Yatefield Mill is situated within seven minutes walk of Rosegrove and Barracks Railway Stations.

Burnley Express, 15 October 1938:

Work for a Thousand. Yatefield Mill formerly one of the largest spinning and weaving centres in the town will shortly be converted for the manufacture of shoes and slippers if the Ministry of Health sanction is obtained for its reconditioning. Should consent be given by the Ministry, and the industry established at the mill, it is estimated that work will eventually be found for a thousand people. A well-known shoe and slipper firm has been in negotiation with the Corporation for some time through the Development Sub Committee, and arrangements are so advanced that steps to complete them are dependant on the Ministry approving a suggested rental and according permission to the Corporation to undertake financial obligations in the adaptations of the premises. The mill, which has been in the procession of the Corporation for some time, will require the expenditure of some thousands of pounds to make it suitable for the proposed requirements. As in the case of many other entire new industries which have been brought to the town, operatives will have to be trained, and possibly at the start numbers engaged will not be great.

When production gets into its stride up to a thousand operatives will probably be provided with work. Burnley people who recall the prosperity enjoyed by Yatefield Mill in its cotton days will hope that the shoe and slipper venture will restore something of the former prestige as a hive of employment. The mill, which was owned by the Haslam Brothers, who also had premises at Colne and ran a wine merchants business in Manchester Road at the corner of Hargreaves Street as a side line, was once one of the town's largest spinning and weaving factories. The firm also had a spinning mill in Aqueduct Street, upon the site of which the Corporations' new transport garage will be erected. The firm had a very high reputation for the quality of its products and the employment which it afforded. It was last run as a cotton mill about ten years ago. The machinery was sold off and the building acquired by the Corporation in its connections with its scheme to get new industries into town.

At the close of the last century the mill figured in a dispute still remembered which, according to the reports and records of the Weavers' Association, saw the expenditure in strike pay of £10,827 17s 10d. The last payment made to the strikers was on 4 February 1899. A retired weaver told an *Express* reporter that when he was a boy people in the Accrington Road and Gannow Districts thought that their future was assured if they got work at Yatefield Mill. 'It was a first-class firm and well managed, and when it closed down it was a matter of great regret,' he said.